"As NFL writers, we often click off our recorders when players begin to delve into their faith, largely unwilling to carry that message to the masses in any meaningful way. In *Men of Sunday*, however, Curtis Eichelberger uses his wide array of NFL sources, graceful writing, and consistently unique perspective on stories to breathe new life into the topic. Through his impeccable lens, Eichelberger reveals in incredible detail a side of the nation's number one sport that is often mentioned but seldom truly examined. In doing so, he teaches us so much more about the men we watch for three hours every fall Sunday but—until now—never truly knew."

—Sam Farmer, NFL Columnist for the *Los Angeles Times*

"Dedicating one's life to God and playing the violent game of professional football would seem a contradiction. But Curtis Eichelberger explains how and why it is not in his book, *Men of Sunday*. In a brilliant narrative, Eichelberger explores how some of the sport's biggest names—Mike Singletary, Reggie White, LaDainian Tomlinson, Ray Lewis, and more—have been able to dedicate their Sundays both to their God and to their careers. Faith can both survive and thrive under the helmet."

—Rick Gosselin, Sports Columnist for the *Dallas Morning News*
Member of the Pro Football Hall of Fame Selection Committee

"*Men of Sunday* is a real, authentic, and honest look into the lives of players, coaches, and wives of the NFL. I was drawn into the stories, the hurt, the pain, the challenge, and the realities of those who make their livelihood by playing football on Sunday. Curtis Eichelberger has made a strong and timely contribution to our understanding of the movement of God that has been growing for years throughout the NFL. I am so thankful for Curtis and this book!"

—Mark Householder, President of Athletes in Action

D0391309

"NFL players have money, fame, and adoring fans, but for the Christian athletes who roam football fields on Sundays, faith is more important and lasting. With feeling and keen insight, Curtis Eichelberger shows how their belief in God's plan helps them deal with the challenges of family, leadership, and crisis as they navigate a world that doesn't always share their values. In *Men of Sunday*, he delves into questions unique to football: Does God really want me to violently hit an opponent? Eichelberger comes up with satisfying answers everyone can use."

—Rick Morrissey, Columnist for the *Chicago Sun-Times*

"A sensitive look at the spiritual lives of the men who risk their bodies on Sundays while offering their souls to God."

— Aaron Kuriloff, NFL Writer for *Bloomberg News*

"The ties between football and religion are strong even though the news media often undervalue the connection. Curtis Eichelberger does an outstanding job of exploring that union on numerous levels. *Men of Sunday* is a must-read for those who want to understand how strongly faith plays a role in the NFL games they watch each season."

—Alex Marvez, Senior NFL Writer for FOXSports.com

MEN
of
SUNDAY

MEN

of

SUNDAY

HOW FAITH GUIDES THE PLAYERS, COACHES & WIVES OF THE NFL

CURTIS EICHELBERGER

THOMAS NELSON
Since 1798

NASHVILLE   DALLAS   MEXICO CITY   RIO DE JANEIRO

Published in Nashville, Tennessee, by Thomas Nelson. Thomas Nelson is a registered trademark of Thomas Nelson, Inc.

Thomas Nelson, Inc. titles may be purchased in bulk for educational, business, fund-raising, or sales promotional use. For information, please e-mail SpecialMarkets@ThomasNelson.com.

Unless otherwise noted, Scripture quotations are taken from the Holy Bible, New International Version®, NIV®. © 1973, 1978, 1984, 2011 by Biblica, Inc.™ Used by permission of Zondervan. All rights reserved worldwide. www.zondervan.com.

Scripture quotations marked KJV are taken from the King James Bible.

Library of Congress Cataloging-in-Publication Data

Eichelberger, Curtis.
  Men of Sunday : how faith guides the players, coaches, and wives of the NFL / Curtis Eichelberger.
    p. cm.
  ISBN 978-0-8499-4734-6 (trade paper)
  1. Football players—Religious life. 2. Football players' spouses—Religious life.
  3. Football coaches—Religious life. 4. National Football League. I. Title.
  BV4596.F6E33 2012
  277.3'08308879633—dc23   2012020233

Printed in the United States of America

12 13 14 15 16 QG 9 8

To my wife, Judit. It was your love, patience, and support that made this project possible.

CONTENTS

CONTENTS

FOREWORD

The National Football League is the most popular sports league in America. Every Sunday in the Fall, millions of people attend a game or watch one on television. The big hits, scintillating runs, precision throws, and acrobatic catches furnish the awe; while an eighty-yard, last-minute scoring drive provides the simulated real-life drama that inspires even the unathletic to believe anything is possible.

The league is so successful that it does not need personalities to prime its popularity. Unlike the NBA, the NHL, or MLB, the NFL is an association of teams whose employees, by necessity, must employ a face mask while they perform their duties, making facial recognition difficult at best. *Men of Sunday* removes the mask from some of the most prominent gridiron greats to give the reader a window into their spiritual journey. Off the field, both coach and player are the everyman. He has health concerns and family issues. His duty to his profession stretches his relationships. To be sure, he generally has significantly more financial means to address his concerns, but material resources can't fix every problem.

Men of Sunday does a masterful job of providing very personal cameos, unveiling these superhuman performers' humanity. It is a rarity for any high-level athlete to show vulnerability. Even rarer is for said athlete to reveal proof of normalcy to an unacquainted author who could leverage his weakness into tabloid-like fodder. *Amazing* is the only word to describe the trust these men have given author Curtis Eichelberger. Equally as stunning is the sensitivity with which he writes each story. Coaches, players, and wives are surprisingly honest as they recount both victories and defeats that cannot be tabulated on a scoreboard.

Eichelberger records lessons on how to maintain a trust-filled marriage when a road-warrior husband is the target of many gold-digging women. He also details how God has journeyed with families through the valley of devastating financial difficulty. He leaves very few stones unturned, lifting even those that uncover the pain of loss unbearable by the unspiritual. Curtis wonderfully allows their story to unfold within its original context and without embellishment. In so doing, the reader is introduced not only to the storyteller but to the Storymaker. Each person's intentional application of biblical truth reveals a spiritual foundation whose cornerstone is Christ.

Every page of *Men of Sunday* has great value. In it, there is help for the common man who is searching for meaning in the mess he has made of his life. There is gained perspective for the NFL employee who does not see the relevancy of God to his occupation. Lastly, there is benefit for the significant others who are both blessed and bothered by the profession their loved one has chosen.

Men of Sunday gives a real and inspiring view of how players, and their families, weave Jesus Christ through the rest of their week. All would do well to take notes.

—Brett Fuller, Washington Redskins Pastor

INTRODUCTION

I n the fall of 2006, I was preparing to write about Joe Gibbs's second stint as head coach of the Washington Redskins when I came across something surprising. Gibbs was producing a Christian video blog each week from his office at Redskins Park. The three-time Super Bowl champion and member of the Pro Football Hall of Fame would sit in front of a camera and discuss the problems he faced coaching the team in postings given titles such as "Power in Our Weakness" and "Life Is a Team Sport." He'd incorporate a Bible lesson in the blog that would help clarify his personal crisis in a way the viewer could relate to. I was so enthralled that I convinced my editors at *Bloomberg News* to let me pursue a story about the role faith played in America's most popular sport. I had covered the NFL for more than a decade, and while I'd interviewed Christian superstars like Green Bay Packers defensive lineman Reggie White and St. Louis Rams quarterback Kurt Warner many times, I was still taken aback by how integrated Christianity had become in the world of professional football. Think about it. An NFL coach was making a Christian video diary from his office. A generation earlier, he'd have been run out of town on rails. Back in the day, NFL teams referred to these men as "Bible Bangers," as you'll learn from Philadelphia Eagles coach Andy Reid in *Men of Sunday*, and considered them weak and soft. But this was Joe Gibbs, one of the greatest coaches in league history, and no one was about to question his toughness.

The more I thought about it, the more I realized it wasn't just Gibbs's blog, or the way more athletes seemed to be caught on camera pointing to the sky after a touchdown pass, or how many are increasingly taking a moment to thank God before beginning a press conference. There was a systematic shift that had gradually taken place over the past decade that reached far beyond a handful of individuals. NFL owners had brought in chaplains to deal with everything from teaching the Bible, to helping players and their families cope with drug and alcohol abuse, infidelity, domestic violence, personal finances, and parenting. NFL players aren't any different from the rest of us, but their problems are magnified a thousandfold. While most married men will be tempted by the seductive lure of a woman outside their family, few will have beautiful twentysomethings trying to climb through their bedroom windows as New York Giants defensive end Justin Tuck explains in chapter 5, "Temptation." And while everyone, man or woman, has work-related stress, none of us will ever have eighty thousand people looking over our shoulders to judge the worthiness of our spreadsheets, debate whether we're worth our salary, or question our intelligence on morning talk radio. The primary tenets of Christianity—discipline, self-sacrifice, courage, and love for one another—aren't just elements of a righteous life; they are the building blocks of good teams and winning franchises, as coaches like Marvin Lewis, Chan Gailey, Tony Dungy, and Brad Childress will attest to in the opening chapter.

When I started working on this book in the summer of 2011 and began interviewing players, coaches, and chaplains, I quickly learned that five years after I stumbled across Gibbs's blog, the role that faith in God played in the NFL had become even more pronounced. A growing cadre of players was suddenly willing to speak out about their faith in God and His role in shaping their lives.

"It's not taboo to say that I am a Christian, and I play football," said Washington Redskins Pro Bowl linebacker London Fletcher. "More guys are talking about it, and with the response the fans and media are giving them now, it's not frowned upon."

Football fans can imagine players getting taped, putting on their pads and pants, psyching themselves up, and marching down the long walk under the stands and onto the playing field for the big game. But what they don't envision, and what is just as important to many of the NFL's greatest stars, is the role prayer plays in those final moments before they sprint onto the field to the roar of the crowd, music, fireworks, and applause. It's then, when we fans are caught up in the spectacle of all the NFL's drama, that many of our heroes stop and pray to God for protection from injury, for help performing to the best of their abilities, and with a promise to do it all in the name of Jesus Christ.

Of all the chapters in this book, the chapter on the violent nature of the game was the most impactful for me because it cut to the heart of the competitor, regardless of his or her profession. It is in this chapter that former Chicago Bears linebacker Mike Singletary and New York Giants defensive lineman Justin Tuck address the question: Can a competitor—on an athletic field, in a courtroom, or in a sales meeting—go for the jugular and still be a good Christian?

This is a story about NFL players and the obstacles they face, but once you take away the cameras and all the bling, their lives are no different than any of ours. In chapter 8, "God's Plan," Tony Dungy and Tennessee Titans quarterback Matt Hasselbeck speak of their struggles to understand the path the Lord has chosen for them. Who among us hasn't battled disappointment and confusion in difficult times and struggled to trust that God has a plan for each of us?

Former Baltimore Ravens quarterback Trent Dilfer pours out his heart about the lessons God imparted to him over the death of his five-year-old son Trevin, in a chapter on the adversity NFL players endure in their personal lives. In perhaps the most heart-wrenching story in *Men of Sunday*, the former Super Bowl quarterback forces the reader to confront the pain God Himself must have endured at the sight of His Son suffering and dying on the cross.

Arizona Cardinals spouses meet for a wives-only Bible study in chapter 3, "Family Sacrifices." Players get cut, injured, and traded, and most contracts aren't guaranteed. Many NFL wives have abandoned their own career aspirations to follow their husbands' dreams. They become professional movers, family nurses, confidence builders, and financial planners. You don't have to be a professional football player to benefit from the lessons team chaplains impart to wives in this chapter on marriage, fidelity, and child rearing.

I close the book with a chapter on leadership, and who better to focus on than Baltimore Ravens linebacker Ray Lewis? The former Super Bowl Most Valuable Player built his own leadership style around the tenets of Christianity and God's teachings. Here, we learn that leadership starts with serving others, not giving commands. Lewis says: Master your craft, help those around you, share the Word of God, and live genuinely so others know your words are true.

Some of our greatest players and coaches reach into the Bible for an instructional word or inspiration in the moments before and after they leave the playing field. Lewis, in the twilight of his career, did just that following the Ravens' 23–20 loss to the New England Patriots in the AFC championship game following the 2011 season, when he stepped to the middle of a despondent Ravens locker room and reminded his teammates: "God doesn't make mistakes. . . . Good will come from this."

Perhaps at no time during the season are faith and the role it plays in building teams more celebrated than at the annual Super Bowl breakfast held the Saturday before the championship. The event is organized by Athletes in Action—a nonprofit organization that uses sports to spread the message of Jesus Christ—and regularly sells out. In 2012, more than two thousand attended the breakfast and silent auction held before the New York Giants beat the New England Patriots 21–17 in Super Bowl XLVI in Indianapolis. It's an officially sponsored NFL event where the Bart Starr Award is given to the NFL player who best exemplifies outstanding character and leadership in his home, on the field, and in the community. Though attendees come from all walks of life, it's largely a religious gathering where Pro Bowl and Hall of Fame players speak of the day they were saved or how it changed their lives. Their testimony is paired with game highlights from their careers, there is a question-and-answer session with Bart Starr, and past winners of the award are sometimes asked to speak. This past year's breakfast started with Kansas City Chiefs owner Clark Hunt giving the invocation and ended with emcee Brent Jones, a former San Francisco 49ers four-time Pro Bowl tight end and television analyst, offering a prayer for those who wished to give their lives to Christ right there in the Indiana State Fairgrounds Exposition Hall.

No matter their skin color, hometown, level of education, physical appearance, or career choice, most all of the breakfast attendees shared a love of Christ and pro football in a way that created a great camaraderie and feeling of warmth at the gathering.

Sundays in the fall have always had a special place among my childhood memories, as they probably do for most of you. We'd go to Sunday school in the morning, drive home, change out of our "church" clothes, wolf down a sandwich, and run to the basement where we'd sit in front of the fireplace and watch the Washington Redskins football game.

It was like that for many families in my hometown, where all the kids had a Joe Theismann jersey, a few autographs from Redskins training camp in their sock drawer, and an Art Monk poster on the wall. Our experience wasn't unique; this scene still plays out all over America, with families from New York to San Diego waking for church and returning home to watch their favorite National Football League team.

This connection between football and faith is something that millions of Americans can connect to and is likely still a part of their weekly dedication.

I was an acolyte during my teen years at Washington Square United Methodist Church in Hagerstown, Maryland; and during the service, I'd have to stay attentive so I'd know when to light the candles and help pass the collection plate. Reverend Louis Emerick, our pastor who retired several years ago, was one of the nicest, most loving people I've ever known, and whether he was a Redskins fan or just intent on keeping his congregation from dozing off, he would usually throw in a reference to the Redskins during his sermons, always eliciting a smile or a nod of approval, as he made some point about love or forgiveness—even when it was directed at those ungodly heathens in Dallas.

No one at my church was holier than thou. We were just ordinary folks. The congregation had its share of drinkers and bad parents, rocky marriages and teenagers who would use the Sunday school sleepover to make out in the nursery room's toy closet. Mostly, we were flawed people, who tried to live a godly life, showed up for church to ask for forgiveness and a do-over the next week . . . and who loved our Redskins.

A common Sunday prayer might go: "Dear God, please make the wind blow behind Mark Moseley's field goals, and don't help the defense any when they are chasing Joe today. I'll try and be better next week."

That's who this book is written for. Just normal folks, football people who go to church on Sunday, come home to root for their team, and live a righteous life . . . most days.

1

TO GLORIFY THE LORD

Do you not know that in a race all the runners run, but only one gets the prize? Run in such a way as to get the prize. Everyone who competes in the games goes into strict training. They do it to get a crown that will not last, but we do it to get a crown that will last forever. Therefore I do not run like someone running aimlessly; I do not fight like a boxer beating the air. No, I strike a blow to my body and make it my slave so that after I have preached to others, I myself will not be disqualified for the prize.

—1 Corinthians 9:24–27

It is a Sunday afternoon in early September and the San Diego Chargers have six minutes before they take the field. Now in full uniform, with their bodies taped and black under their eyes, they are laser focused when defensive end Jacques Cesaire calls out, "Pray It Up." Between twenty-five and thirty players put away their iPods and give pictures of their children a final kiss. Their cleats *click-clack* as they march into the tiled shower room, their shoulder pads bump as they gather together, the smell of sweat permeates the space. Then team chaplain Shawn Mitchell leads them in prayer.

It is here that some of the greatest athletes of our time will pray to God for protection from injury, for the safety of their adversaries, for the strength and ability to execute and play to the best of their God-given talents, and to do it all in the name of the Lord.

This scene is played out in locker rooms around the National Football League every Sunday outside the view of television cameras, opponents, and critics. It is a rallying moment for the men as they clasp hands and make final preparations, players say.

"They have been preparing all week and there is this sense that, 'OK, here it comes,'" says Mitchell. "Prayer is not a rabbit's foot or a superstition. We are talking to a God who cares for every facet of our lives. If it is important to them, it is important to God."

The adrenaline is running high. The players are emotional. It's difficult to discipline themselves to quiet down for Pray-Up.

"What I like to tell the guys is, 'Pray like everything depends on God because it does, and then perform like everything depends on you,'" says Mitchell.

While the players continue shuffling into the confined space of the shower, network television analysts sit in a small room at the top of the stadium updating viewers on injuries, weather conditions, and key matchups. The singer who will perform the national anthem is pacing near the end zone, sipping water and whispering the song. Field crews are checking the sidelines to make sure medical kits and water bottles are in place. And fans at home are making their final runs to the refrigerator, stacking an extra hot dog on their paper plates, opening a beer, teasing their brother-in-law about his fantasy league picks.

And in that moment when the outside world is enjoying the company of family and friends, enraptured by the pageantry of what has become a rite of fall, thirty men dressed in armor like modern-day gladiators stand together, holding hands in the bowels of the stadium, awaiting a final moment with the Lord before the game. Then, silence.

"Father, we thank You for this opportunity where we can come together as one . . . ," Mitchell prays.

"We bow our heads together for what is before us and, Lord, You have made it clear that apart from You we can do nothing, but with You all things are possible . . .

"Lord, we expect big things from You, so today we go out to attempt great things for You . . .

"Our desire is to lift You up to glorify You . . .

"We ask that You keep both teams free of injury . . .

"And we ask, Lord, that we can go out there and perform to the greatest of our God-given ability . . .

"We pray for the strength of Samson, the speed of Jehu, and give us awareness and instinct . . .

"We go forth from here in Your name, use us now, we thank You in advance, in Jesus' name. Amen."

For all that the National Football League represents to the millions of fans who watch the games around the world, the role faith plays in the lives of the players has been largely overlooked by media outlets that don't want to offend nonbelievers, see faith as a personal choice, or don't want to be used by false Christians looking to shine up their public image.

When Mitchell concludes Pray-Up with "Amen," the players march back out of the shower to the locker room, though some stay behind for an additional minute to get a word or a personal prayer with Mitchell. Sometimes players recite lines of Scripture to reaffirm their faith and calm themselves before entering the stadium. Other times, they just speak to God straight from the heart.

PREGAME PRAYERS

Some of the sport's biggest stars are also some of its most faithful. Players like Green Bay Packers quarterback Aaron Rodgers, New

Orleans Saints quarterback Drew Brees, Pittsburgh Steelers safety Troy Polamalu, Tennessee Titans quarterback Matt Hasselbeck, and Baltimore Ravens linebacker Ray Lewis, to name just a few.

Each player prepares for the game in his own way.

In San Diego, as Mitchell's prayer concludes, Chargers offensive tackle Jeromey Clary keeps his head bowed and prays, "Allow me to glorify You in all that You've done. Protect me and allow me to play with strength and confidence, yet stay humble. The glory is Yours."

In St. Louis, Rams quarterback Sam Bradford has prepared spiritually for games dating back to his college years at the University of Oklahoma by reading the story of David and Goliath about a young boy who slays a battle-tested warrior with a slingshot. In 1 Samuel 17:45–46, David declares, "You come against me with sword and spear and javelin, but I come against you in the name of the LORD Almighty, the God of the armies of Israel, whom you have defied. This day the LORD will deliver you into my hands, and I'll strike you down and cut off your head."

In Tennessee, Titans quarterback Matt Hasselbeck gathers with the team's other passers in the stadium tunnel minutes before they take the field for what they call the Quarterbacks Prayer.

It started when he played in Seattle alongside fellow Christians Trent Dilfer and quarterbacks coach Jim Zorn. The prayer isn't scripted, Hasselbeck says, but it goes something like this:

> God, there are so many people counting on us today: our team-mates, our coaches, our families, the people in the stands. I pray that we wouldn't look for their approval. I pray that we look for Your approval; that we play for an audience of one today. And knowing that we've worked hard and prepared, I pray that You'd slow things down and give us a peace that can only come from You, and take that pressure and burden off us so we can go out and play knowing that at the end of the day, win, lose, or draw, You did that.

We pray that we make the most of our God-given abilities. God, I need Your help. Please walk with me today. In Your name. Amen.

Prayer isn't the domain of offensive players. Some of the nastiest hitters in the NFL stop to worship God before taking the field.

In East Rutherford, New Jersey, New York Giants Pro Bowl defensive end Justin Tuck takes a knee at the end of the bench before kickoff to ask God to protect him from injury.

In Washington, safety Oshiomogho Atogwe reads passages from the Twenty-third Psalm and prays: "God, I thank You for allowing me the week of preparation. Let me be confident in what I'm doing. Let me lead my teammates and encourage them. But more than that, let me glorify You with the way I play, with my attitude, with my energy, and let me give You my all."

And in Baltimore, Ray Lewis's mother, Buffy Jenkins, has been sending a line of Scripture for her son to read before games since he entered the league in 1996. It usually has something to do with the moment, Lewis says. One example comes from Psalm 16:1–2: "Keep me safe, my God, for in you I take refuge. I say to the LORD, 'You are my Lord; apart from you I have no good thing.'"

Back in the Chargers locker room, players now have a few minutes to adjust their equipment before strength coach Jeff Hurd enters the room and shouts, "Two minutes!" It's coming now. Now! The intensity in the locker room ramps up. This is it. Coach Norv Turner barks out: "OK, men, let's gather around." The players take a knee, everyone grabs a teammate's hand, and Turner leads the group in the Lord's Prayer:

> *Our Father which art in heaven, Hallowed be thy name.*
> *Thy kingdom come, Thy will be done in earth, as it is in heaven.*
> *Give us this day our daily bread.*
> *And forgive us our debts, as we forgive our debtors.*
> *And lead us not into temptation, but deliver us from evil: For*

thine is the kingdom, and the power, and the glory, for ever.
Amen. (Matthew 6:9–13 KJV)

There is a pause afterward, and then Turner gives a short pre-game speech meant to inspire the players and send them onto the field focused on key strategies. Much is at risk, and the players know it. For some, it's about keeping their place on the team. For others, it's about accomplishing some personal or team goal, maintaining their income, making their families proud, or using their skills to glorify God. No matter their motivation, one thing is certain: time is running out. The average NFL career lasts 3.5 years, according to the NFL union, and if the players are going to make it in this game, they'll have to do something big in the next few moments.

BUILDING BETTER TEAMS

No doubt, there is a lot riding on what happens Sunday afternoons. But game day only highlights a small part of an NFL player's or coach's religious life. Faith plays a role in everything from the draft to retirement, from single living to marriage, and from the time they are injured through their recovery.

For NFL teams, the chapel services, Bible studies, and religious instruction are both supportive and self-serving. The teams are providing a way for men of faith to attend chapel and continue their religious education year-round. But it's also an inexpensive social service that provides the sort of counseling and therapy that keeps players mentally and emotionally at the top of their game and ready to compete.

"I think that having a chapel service or an organized way of worshiping is a good thing," says Dallas Cowboys owner Jerry Jones. "Your chaplain or pastor associates with players throughout the year, providing a very significant service in times of need and with other private issues. I don't think there's any question it's an asset to have a program in place, as long as everybody knows they are going of their own volition and the team isn't requiring they attend a particular service. I'm very sensitive about that."

Washington Redskins owner Dan Snyder, who has one of the most involved chaplains in the league in Pastor Brett Fuller, agrees with Jones. While the decision to worship rests with each individual player, Snyder sees it as his responsibility as an owner to ensure religious guidance is available for those who desire it. It's part of team building, he says.

"My philosophy as an NFL owner has always been to provide support to the coaches and players both on and off of the field," Snyder says. "Having strong spiritual advisers is a key aid in the success of our team."

Religious services vary from one team to the next, usually depending on the coach. Cleveland Browns chaplain Tom Petersburg says Sam Rutigliano, who coached the team to two play-off appearances between 1978 and 1984, was so happy his players were meeting for Bible study that he would send them pizzas.

Other coaches, though, even those who were devout Christians, were afraid religion would divide the locker room, and they would limit Petersburg's access to the players. Each team's religious practices are a reflection of the coach, chaplains say, and because eight to ten clubs fire their head coach each year, faith-based offerings vary from one season to the next.

To fully understand the impact religion has on NFL teams, one has to understand how coaches and chaplains view the role of religion and why it is so important to the clubs.

Former coach Tony Dungy, who led the Indianapolis Colts to a Super Bowl championship after the 2006 season and now works as an analyst for NBC Sports, never hid his strong religious beliefs from his players, his owner, or the public. In fact, he said that he could no more separate his beliefs in God from his job coaching a football team than separate his head from his body. His faith dictated how he led his life and how he built his roster.

That included choosing players who were a "good fit" for the franchise. Sometimes, those were "character guys" rather than the most talented players on the training camp roster, he says.

"I had to do what in my heart was the right thing to do, and my Christian beliefs were going to guide those decisions," Dungy says. "The Bible clearly says you are living in the world, so you can't expect to have an all-Christian team and staff. You have to do what's best for the team and draft the best players. But because of my beliefs, that's not always about taking the most physically talented guy. We took a lot of guys off the draft board because we didn't think they would fit in with what we were trying to do," he says. "I told the team, 'We are not going to sit here and pray about everything, and I don't expect you all to believe exactly what I believe, but here is how I'm going to make decisions, and what I am going to do with my life.'"

Coaches point out that faith is a steadying influence in a league where careers, marriages, friendships, and self-identity can be shattered by one wrong twist of a knee or one bad season. The newly rich, self-confident, and celebrated NFL players posing for pictures with their adoring fans are far more insecure and vulnerable behind closed locker room doors than they appear in public, coaches and team chaplains say. Many turn to their religious upbringing for greater balance in their lives. Others like the way it brings them closer to their fellow teammates and builds camaraderie.

"I thought it was interesting when I got into the league that we started and finished every game with the Lord's Prayer," says Green Bay quarterback Aaron Rodgers. "Growing up in the evangelical Christian church, it's not something that you really learn as a kid, so I kind of learned the Lord's Prayer on the fly as a rookie.

"I enjoy the intertwine of sports and religion," he says. "A lot of guys come from religious backgrounds, so there's that familiarity there, and it is fun to be able to pray with your teammates before and after games."

Current and former NFL coaches, including Dungy, former Washington Redskins coach Joe Gibbs, Cincinnati Bengals coach Marvin Lewis, Philadelphia Eagles coach Andy Reid, and Minnesota Vikings coach Leslie Frazier, agree that team ministries can play a crucial role in building a winning franchise. Most teams offer chapel services, Bible studies, couples Bible studies for players and their wives or girlfriends, and one-on-one counseling sessions for anyone in the organization who needs help with a personal problem.

Team chaplains often come to teams through their relationships with nonprofit groups like Athletes in Action or Fellowship of Christian Athletes. Some chaplains are provided with an office and midweek locker room access, while others appear only on game days. It differs from one coach to the next, with some wanting a chaplain to provide religious guidance, while others see faith as a personal issue to be dealt with on a player's own time. Though team chaplains are usually Christian, most clubs offer to contact a rabbi, cleric, or other religious leader if a player requests one. The help these chaplains provide goes way beyond the on-field product fans see on Sundays.

"One of the greatest impacts our chaplains have on the NFL is when we help players understand how to be solid husbands and fathers, and how to protect their families," says Corwin Anthony, national director of pro ministry for Athletes in Action. "When you have stability at home and are at peace with the way you are living your life, it really makes a big difference."

Many coaches, like the Buffalo Bills' Chan Gailey, remark that a chaplain might not get drafted number one, but his function within the team can be just as important.

"I think they do a good job of keeping guys down to earth," says Gailey. "When things get bad, they are able to regulate that by reminding them there are other things in life to be positive about. And when things are going good, it keeps them level-headed."

According to Cleveland Browns chaplain Tom Petersburg, off-the-field troubles can ruin a player's career as much as a torn knee ligament or broken ankle. "I [Petersburg] had a player come to me once and say, 'My marriage is a mess, and I'm a mess. I cannot perform on Sunday unless I get straightened out here. What do I do?'" Burdens occupying the players' minds can include money, women, pressure to perform, family demands, friends wanting to borrow money, or injuries they don't want to reveal to the team out of fear their coach will replace them in the lineup.

And it goes even further than that.

FAMILIES, TEAMS SHARE CORE VALUES

Every coach asserts that he wants great athletes who are good citizens and team players. Who wouldn't? Oftentimes, though, great talent comes at a cost to the player and, ultimately, the team, by way of pride, ego, greed, and selfishness. And to a point, teams have to tolerate those character traits in order to build winning teams and fill stadiums. Is it any different in a corporate sales office or executive locker room where bad citizens are tolerated because they are rainmakers?

Dungy says that he tried to impart the same wisdom and advice to his players that he gave to his own children. Many of those pep talks were based on Dungy's religious beliefs and Christianity's core values of sacrifice, self-restraint, and helping others. Those qualities don't just build better people, he says; they build better teams. He noticed that players who believed in the tenets of the Christian faith often exhibited the qualities he was trying to instill in the franchise as a whole.

"I believe you win by sacrificing," Dungy says. "By saying there are some things I could do, but for the good of the others on the team, I'm not going to. People who do that in life will probably do that on the football field for you. So if I tell a receiver that I'll need him to do a lot of blocking this week and he might only catch one ball, it's my experience that a person who I've seen sacrifice in other areas of his life is more likely to do it on the football field too."

Not every coach agrees with Dungy's religious perspective. With all due respect to his 139-69 regular season record, nineteen postseason appearances, and Super Bowl championship, some think a bolder line of demarcation has to be drawn between religion and football.

Buffalo Bills coach Chan Gailey says that he has a strong faith in God, but that he doesn't want to confuse the players or leave them feeling that they might be treated unfairly.

"If a guy wants to know about Christ and he walks in my office, I'll be happy to tell him. But I'm not going to beat him over the head with the Bible," Gailey states.

While most Christians would agree that they wouldn't want a Muslim boss trying to convert them every day, doesn't the Bible call for God's disciples to spread the Word?

We read in Matthew 28:18–20: "Then Jesus came to them and said, 'All authority in heaven and on earth has been given to me. Therefore go and make disciples of all nations, baptizing them in the name of the Father and of the Son and of the Holy Spirit, and teaching them to obey everything I have commanded you. And surely I am with you always, to the very end of the age.'"

Coaches believe it's a personal call. Some decide to keep religion and football separate, while others quote directly from the Bible.

Leslie Frazier, a former defensive back for the Chicago Bears and now the head coach of the Minnesota Vikings, points out that coaches have often reached into the Bible for help getting their teams through difficult times.

He remembers one occasion in 2007 when he was an assistant to then Minnesota Vikings head coach Brad Childress. The rival Green Bay Packers had beaten the Vikings 34–0, dropping Minnesota to 3-6 on the season and creating a city full of doubters.

With seven games remaining in the regular season, they still had a shot at the play-offs, though you'd never know it by the level of public criticism.

Frazier was in Childress's office after the loss, and the two men discussed the role prayer would play in trying to get the team through the difficulties it faced. They decided to focus on Paul's letter to the Philippians, which he wrote during his imprisonment in Rome, encouraging Christians to be united in one another and think of themselves not as individuals, but as being united in the body of Christ and belonging to each other.

"We focused on finishing the race together," Frazier recalls. "It would be a race of perseverance, and we both prayed in his office that Monday, before he went down and talked to the team. We just wanted to make sure we were both in the right frame of mind before going down there because we felt like our season could go either way.

"He talked about perseverance," Frazier continues, "and the fact that we were going to go through difficult times, much like Paul had in the Scripture and like we were experiencing then."

Childress told the team: "Paul finished the race and that's what we have to do, and the only way is if we unite as a group. It doesn't matter what the media is saying about us right now or how people are picking us apart. We have to join together as one and persevere through a tough storm."

The club reeled off five consecutive wins, before losing its final two, to finish the season a respectable 8-8, though not good enough to make the play-offs. Minnesota would go 10-6 the following season and 12-4 in 2009, qualifying for the play-offs both years. Childress was fired following a 3-7 start to the 2010 season. He was 40-37, including 1-2 in the play-offs, in four and a half years as the Vikings head coach. His best season was 2009 when he guided the team to the NFC Conference championship before losing to the eventual Super Bowl champion New Orleans Saints, 31–28, in overtime.

"I really believe that's kind of where we found out who we were as a team," Frazier says. "We were a team that was going to persevere through an embarrassing time and not let that one loss define us. Scripture helped us get through that moment. It was because of faith and prayer as opposed to saying: 'We're going to roll up our sleeves and fix this.' It was relying on God to show us what direction we needed to take, what words we needed to speak to our players to get them motivated and in the right frame of mind so that we could persevere."

One can't underestimate the value that faith in God has in shaping a player's life and ultimately his NFL team. When a young player starts his pro football career, he's not just establishing himself on the field; he's determining how he is going to live the rest of his days. Who is he as a man? Is he the guy who will spend his evenings partying with women he never establishes a loving relationship with? Will he invest his money in endless rounds of high-stakes poker games or get-rich-quick schemes? Will he be the guy who believes parties are a rite of passage in the NFL, or will he be the guy who returns home to read to his children before their bedtime? What vision of himself does he aspire to? Oftentimes, coaches have said, the answers to these questions will also dictate who he becomes as an NFL player. How long he stays in the league. And what his life looks like when his career ends.

Cincinnati Bengals coach Marvin Lewis believes faith is so important in the development of a young player that when he signs a rookie or free agent, "I'll basically mandate that everyone goes to chapel at least once because I want them to have the experience of it. I'm not going to force my beliefs on them, but it's important for them to know it's not a bad thing; it's a good thing. Then I'll leave it alone. They can't feel pressured. We want the environment to be comfortable to them, but not overbearing. They have a choice."

Like many teams, the Bengals have a chapel service throughout the year, including minicamps and rookie camp. They also offer a Bible study with potluck dinners at players' homes, and they hire a baby-sitting service to watch the kids while the players and their wives attend the meeting. Lewis said he wants the environment to be comfortable and fun rather than overbearing or pressured. But most coaches think that chapel and Bible study are about more than fellowship. It all ties back to their careers and the kind of people they are as players.

FEARLESS, CONFIDENT, TRUSTING

Take injuries, for example. Coaches have noticed that players of faith are often better at responding to personal crisis because they see it as part of God's plan. In any business, coaches say, the best employees aren't the ones who perform like champs during the good times, but instead, those who refuse to quit or dwell on the negative, and who find ways to succeed in the bad times. Where do the inner strength and discipline come from?

"When a player of faith is injured," says Lewis, "and I mean a serious season-ending injury, they're more likely to see it as being part of God's plan and believe, 'There has got to be something good that will come out of this for me.' That's a different way of thinking about an injury or any setback for that matter."

Former Baltimore Ravens coach Brian Billick comments that it's only natural for an injured player to be afraid of being reinjured when he returns. But it's exactly that fear and insecurity that is the worst thing for a player because if he's timid or protective of the injury, it actually increases the likelihood of reinjury as he tries to protect himself.

Billick says when players who have turned their lives over to God return from injury, they are oftentimes fearless because it is not in their hands. It is in God's hands, and that is a big relief. Former Vikings coach Brad Childress recalls that is exactly the type of response he received from cornerback Cedric Griffin, who tore the anterior cruciate ligament in his left knee in the Vikings' overtime loss in the NFC championship game. Griffin spent that spring and summer in rehabilitation.

"Cedric's a faith guy," declares Childress. "That's how NFL coaches refer to players who have strong religious beliefs. They'll say, 'He's a faith guy.'

"He could be a sourpuss right now, a woe-is-me type, asking God, 'Why would You do this to me?' But I know he is a believer, and that's not the box he is going to put himself in. He's going to work his tail off and have faith. No excuses. No crying. That's not uncommon with these guys," Childress says of players of faith.

It goes beyond just injuries, though.

Chan Gailey coached the Dallas Cowboys in 1998 and 1999, guiding them to the play-offs both years. He was fired and landed at Georgia Tech (2002–7), where he became the first coach in school history to lead the Yellow Jackets to bowl games in his first six seasons. After a stint in Kansas City as the Chiefs' offensive coordinator, Gailey was hired to coach the Buffalo Bills in January 2010.

"God is in control of the big picture. Your responsibility is to take the talent and ability you have been given and do the best you can with them each and every time you walk out there on the field," Gailey says. "That's it. That's all you're responsible for. Having that faith really helps guys through the ups and downs."

It's not just the players who benefit. It's the coaches too. According to Gailey, his experience coaching college and professional football has convinced him that his belief in Christ has allowed him to remain in the profession and stitch together a successful career.

"I've learned through years of experience that your belief in Christ is the thing that allows you to go to work every day because if you didn't have that, you'd be trying to please too many people and you'd be blown by the wind or you'd make decisions based upon popular opinion or something else that's not what is right and good for everyone involved on that day," Gailey says. "If your faith is strong, the job isn't pressure packed. That's the point. I'm going to get up today and do the best I can. I'm not worried about pleasing fans or pleasing players. I have to please Him, and that's the only thing I've got to do. You can get caught up in all the other stuff. Yeah, the pressure is hard, but all it can do is kill me. If the worst that happens to me is they kill me, I'm all right; I'm going to heaven. They can't hurt me. I worry more about somebody saying something to my family than what they say about me.

"I pray that I will honor God with my life. That's what I pray for. I want His wisdom and His strength and His power and His discernment to filter through me, and if you have a close enough walk with Him, it will.

"Sometimes I mess it up, but He doesn't. And I just pray that I would honor Him with my life, and the only way you honor Him is you listen to His Word only, you obey His Word only, and you look for approval from Him only, and if I can do that on a daily basis, then I think I have a chance to make quality decisions for everybody involved."

When a player is a "faith guy," it's usually pretty obvious. He tends to be less self-centered, and coaches and teammates tend to see him in chapel and Bible study. Sometimes, though, players use faith to deceive, and nothing burns believers more than that.

Childress says he would use a player's religious beliefs as a test of his character and honesty. If he lies about something as personal as his faith, can he be trusted on the field? Can he be believed when there is a problem in the community?

So when Childress would meet with his players during the off-season, he would have them write down their values as a way of understanding the player and what's important to him. Typically, Childress says, guys are going to list their faith and their family as numbers one and two. They also might say building wealth or developing a good reputation or being a good friend.

"I tell them, 'All right, but don't put those things down there because Coach Childress wants to hear those things. Tell me the truth. What are your values? Is it honesty? Is it being tough-minded? Is it having fun? Is it being a good father and provider? There are all kinds of things when you talk about what your values are. What's important is: Are you who you say you are? You can't put down faith and family if you are a married father with a couple kids and you are spending a whole bunch of time in a strip club.' And I give them that example. 'Don't put that down,' I say. 'You are not trying to inspire me.' I have a whole stack of three-by-five cards on my desk over here, so I know when a guy comes in and he has said faith is one of his values. I say to him, 'How are you doing in your walk [with God]?'

"I think we have a culture of truth here. If you want to know where you stand, I don't have any problem letting you know. But you have to be honest with me too. And I'm listening and paying attention, and I'll follow up to see if you are living the life that you say you are. That's a measure of a man's character. And when you have been beaten on, and you are so tired you can barely lift your legs and the fans are booing and it's late in the game and we are trailing and need to pull it out from somewhere deep inside, that is when a man exposes his character. I need to know what I can expect from him."

Coaches are ultimately responsible for creating faith-based programs like chapel and Bible study and for recognizing them in a way that encourages players to participate without feeling put-upon or forced.

The rest is left to the team chaplains, who must walk a fine line between the players and team management.

LIFE CRISIS

Most coaches instruct their chaplains to help the players spiritually and emotionally and to keep their conversations private unless the health or the life of the player or his family is at risk. They are not to become a distraction to the team or question managerial decisions.

Bengals chaplain Ken Moyer understood this role immediately. The 6-foot-7, 297-pound former offensive lineman played five NFL seasons with the Bengals and had firsthand knowledge of the stress players face every day.

This is a tremendous help to Marvin Lewis, who says the employee/employer relationship isn't any different in the NFL than it is at IBM or General Motors. You don't want your boss to know about your personal problems because you're afraid it could have a big impact on your work and career.

"Players go from starting to not starting," Lewis says. "They are having the season of their career, and then they get injured. They have spousal relationship issues. There are deaths. So there are a lot of things they are really more comfortable sharing with Ken."

During the 2009 season, Bengals defensive coordinator Mike Zimmer's wife, Vikki, died suddenly, and according to Lewis, it affected some of the assistant coaches and players. Then, Bengals receiver Chris Henry fell out the back of a truck and died from injuries he sustained in the fall. "When Chris died, I can't put my finger on where each of those fifty-three players' relationships was with Chris, but Ken could," Lewis admits. "And he could help them deal with that.

"I think that Ken, being a former player, realizes that faith has its place, and we talk about faith and family and football and you can't screw that order up when it's convenient for yourself. In my mind, that's how we are going to operate here. Faith is number one, their family and then football, so when they have a decision to make, I want them to make their decision based on that."

Team chaplains minister to a young, wealthy, and sometimes troubled flock. At the start of the 2011 season, the average NFL player was 26.4 years old and was paid an average of $2.25 million annually, according to the National Football League and its players union. Chaplains say they consider themselves part minister, psychologist, family counselor, and father figure. In private, they address issues from drug and alcohol abuse to infidelity, domestic violence, parenting, financial issues, injury fears, job stress, and conflict resolution with coaches, managers, and wives.

Lewis's experience wasn't uncommon. Joe Gibbs had won three Super Bowls and been voted into the Pro Football Hall of Fame, but nothing had prepared him for the day in 2007 when Sean Taylor, a twenty-four-year-old Pro Bowl safety nicknamed "Meast" because teammates said he was half man, half beast, lay dead in a mahogany coffin at Florida International University, the victim of a robbery gone bad.

Gibbs, a devout Christian, in his second stint coaching the Redskins, was widely known and respected as a man of faith. He'd told the story in countless community meetings of how his egotism and near financial ruin had brought him closer to God. He'd even started a Christian video blog from Redskins headquarters where he used Scripture to provide lessons on the team's struggles in blog postings titled "Avoiding Self-Pity" and "When We Feel Alone" and had given away thousands of Bibles through his website.

But even for him, Taylor's shocking death was hard to handle. Taylor, who'd had his share of personal problems, was beginning to mature. His life changed after he became a father, and he started connecting more with coaches and teammates. He'd even sought out the team's minister. In the days after his death, the team was distraught. "Our chaplains met nonstop with our players and coaches," Gibbs shares. "Sean was strong and athletic and full of life, and then he was gone. Why? And where was he now? Our young players were very uncertain. It forced them to reevaluate their own lives and their own vulnerabilities. It made them, probably for the first time in their lives, ask, 'If something were to happen to me, where would I spend eternity?' They were questions that required deeper thought, and many of them turned to our chaplain."

AS THE CLOCK EXPIRES . . . PLAYERS GATHER FOR PRAYER

The role that faith plays in the NFL cannot be understated. Even though it is one of the most underreported elements of building a good team, it plays a vital role in franchises from San Diego to Washington.

The Chargers started the 2011 season 4-1. Pundits were saying it was time for Coach Norv Turner—who had amassed a 41-23 regular-season record and three AFC West division titles in his first four seasons—to either deliver a Super Bowl or step aside.

As the game in San Diego winds down, fans start gathering their belongings and slowly heading for the exits. On television, the broadcasters begin their wrap-up, running through the stars of the game and thanking members of their crew. And kids are running into their backyards, hoping to play touch football between the hedges before it gets dark and their mothers call them in for dinner.

When the game clock ticks to zero, players of faith from both teams begin assembling around the 50-yard line to say a postgame prayer. Some know one another from when they played for other franchises or from their college days, though many only know one another from their postgame worship. They take a knee, sometimes clasp hands, and bow their heads in prayer.

The purpose of the gathering is to draw attention to themselves, to use the platform they have in front of the tens of thousands of fans still lingering in the stadium to promote their belief in Christ. The hope, says Corwin Anthony, is that some little boy or girl will turn to his or her father and ask: "Daddy, what are they doing?"

Chargers tackle Jeromey Clary, father of a two-year-old son named Cannon, signed a four-year contract shortly after the owners and players negotiated a new labor agreement in the summer of 2011. The 6-foot-6, 320-pound tackle from Mansfield, Texas, won the Ed Block Courage Award in 2010, given to one player on each team who exemplifies commitment to the principles of sportsmanship and courage. It was quite a year. Money, notoriety, respect, and there he was, the epitome of the modern-day pro athlete living out the childhood dreams of millions of ordinary fans . . . down on a knee.

"We've been blessed with talent to play a game for a living, and we use that moment right after the game to thank God for allowing us to do what we do," Clary says. "We thank Him for our health. And we ask Him to watch over the visiting team on their trip home. It's really just a moment after it's all over to take a minute and give thanks to Him."

A VIOLENT GAME

When you go to war against your enemies and see horses and chariots and an army greater than yours, do not be afraid of them, because the LORD your God, who brought you up out of Egypt, will be with you. When you are about to go into battle, the priest shall come forward and address the army. He shall say: "Hear, Israel: Today you are going into battle against your enemies. Do not be fainthearted or afraid; do not panic or be terrified by them. For the LORD your God is the one who goes with you to fight for you against your enemies to give you victory."

—Deuteronomy 20:1–4

It was forty degrees with a stiff wind blowing off Lake Michigan when the Tampa Bay Buccaneers kicked off to the Chicago Bears at Soldier Field on November 19, 1989.

The Bucs were 3-7 and suffering like most years in the 1980s, while the Bears, 6-4, just four seasons removed from their Super Bowl victory, were on the precipice of a six-game losing streak that would send them toward the bottom of their division.

As the game neared the end of the opening quarter, Tampa Bay had the ball first-and-10 on its own 32-yard line when Bucs' quarterback Vinny Testaverde dropped back to pass.

Running back Sylvester Stamps, a sixth-year player out of Jackson State, ran a short pass pattern across the middle and had turned back to make eye contact with Testaverde when—

He never saw it coming.

Chicago Bears middle linebacker Mike Singletary, one of the most ferocious hitters to ever play the position, had spotted the receiver out of the corner of his eye and was running at a dead sprint when Stamps turned back to spot the ball. The collision was brutal. The hit turned Stamps into a crumpled, motionless mass. It was one of those "ooh-ahh" hits that builds a legacy and, in time, sends a man to the Pro Football Hall of Fame.

"His eyes rolled back into his head," Singletary remembers. "His tongue fell out of his mouth. He didn't move."

Singletary was scared. He'd watched hundreds of opponents return to the huddle glassy-eyed, unable to recall their name or the team they played for. But this time was different. He was afraid he might have done real damage.

The linebacker took a knee and began praying.

"No one knew what to say," Singletary says. "It looked bad. And I thought to myself, *What am I doing? Something is wrong with this.* I waited and watched until it looked like he was going to be OK, and then I refocused on my job. We never spoke."

FEAR, PARALYSIS, DEATH

Singletary's hit on Stamps wasn't unique by any means. Hundreds of players have similar collisions every week in the NFL. The league has tried to reduce the number of injuries by changing its rules to protect quarterbacks, defenseless receivers, even members of the kickoff and return teams. But it's a violent game, and these are the risks the players accept.

The NFL is littered with examples of guys who were paralyzed or nearly killed by hard hits. Oakland Raiders safety Jack Tatum, nicknamed "The Assassin," hit New England Patriots receiver Darryl Stingley during an exhibition game at the Oakland Coliseum in 1978 that severed two vertebrae, leaving the receiver paralyzed and in a wheelchair until his death in 2007 at the age of fifty-five. Tatum, who died in 2010 at sixty-one, never apologized because he said it was a clean hit.

A generation later, Buffalo Bills tight end Kevin Everett fell to the ground after tackling Denver Broncos returner Domenik Hixon on a kickoff in September 2007. The helmet-to-helmet collision caused a fracture dislocation of the third and fourth vertebrae and compression of the spinal cord. Initially paralyzed from the neck down, Everett eventually recovered and was able to walk again.

Now that players of Singletary's era are beginning to age, even those who finished their careers relatively healthy need joint replacements and have begun showing signs of brain damage and early-stage dementia—though that hasn't been conclusively linked to football.

Baseball, basketball, hockey, soccer—no other sport seems to have as many religious players practicing their faith as in the NFL, chaplains and coaches report.

Many believe that the violent nature of the game and the non-guaranteed contracts are two of the primary reasons players seek a relationship with God more in the NFL than in other professional sports.

The high injury rate and punishing blows players deliver and receive every week pose important questions for Christian football players and their families from the high school level to the pros. And they are the same questions today that Singletary faced two decades ago.

How can one say he is a man of Christ and still happily participate in one of the most violent games our society has ever known? What's more, how can millions of Christians the world over claim to love it so much? Is it not against God and all that He represents to hit a man so violently that his brain rattles inside his skull and he can no longer function as a human being?

The first month of the 2011 NFL season was a busy time for team doctors. Indianapolis Colts quarterback Kerry Collins and Philadelphia Eagles quarterback Michael Vick suffered concussions, and New York Giants wide receiver Domenik Hixon was lost for the year after tearing the anterior cruciate ligament in his right knee.

It continued into October, when the Oakland Raiders lost quarterback Jason Campbell with a broken collarbone, Buffalo Bills linebacker Shawne Merriman tore his right Achilles tendon, and Houston Texans linebacker Mario Williams tore a pectoral muscle.

In November, Chicago Bears quarterback Jay Cutler (broken thumb) and Kansas City Chiefs quarterback Matt Cassel (hand surgery) were knocked out for the remainder of the season.

And in December, New York Jets safety Jim Leonhard (torn patellar tendon), Dallas Cowboys standout rookie running back DeMarco Murray (broken ankle), and Cleveland Browns quarterback Colt McCoy (concussion) each suffered a serious injury.

By the end of the regular season, 443 players had been placed on injured reserve, according to the NFL union, meaning their injuries were so severe that they couldn't play for the remainder of the season. Almost no player survives an entire sixteen-game regular season without visiting a trainer for some ailment, teams say. It is the nature of the game. And as players get bigger and faster with each successive generation, injuries will probably only increase in number and severity.

No doubt, it's a violent game. But is it *ungodly* violent? Is it against God's wishes to hit an opponent so hard that he has a neurological malfunction? Is it unchristian to celebrate that hit with a teammate and eighty thousand screaming fans? Is it morally wrong for a fan to leap from the couch and high-five her brother or to laugh at a player who stumbles toward the wrong sideline?

These questions, some of which Singletary asked himself in the late 1980s, speak directly to the competitive nature of all Christian men and women. It doesn't matter whether a Christian is chasing a quarterback, negotiating a contract with an inexperienced opponent, or closing a sale at a pharmaceuticals convention. The question is this: As competitors, can we go for the jugular and still be Christlike? And can our supporters cheer our success, knowing that it comes at the expense of one of God's children?

Years after he sent running backs sprawling on their backsides and returning to their huddle babbling incoherently, Singletary found himself at a crossroads: Could he be the Christian he aspired to be and still play the game he loved?

"I was really wrestling over whether I wanted to continue playing the game," Singletary says. "I was thinking, *Lord, I love You so much, and I'm out here hurting people, and I don't want to do that. Am I wrong in what I'm doing? Is this sending the wrong message?*

"I was at a moment in my career where a lot of people were questioning the way I was playing the game. 'This guy is hurting people,' they were saying. I was knocking guys out, and guys were lying on the ground not getting up. And I was like, 'Well, wait a minute, let me think about this.'"

Singletary met privately with friends in the ministry and spent a great deal of time in prayer. He could see in his mind the faces of the countless players he'd taken out over the years. And he knew they were someone's father, someone's husband, someone's son. There was a family out there praying that God would protect their loved one from . . . Mike Singletary.

There was a family that clasped hands in front of a television set, who paced outside a doctor's office, who knelt in prayer asking God to fix the damage that Singletary had done. Was he doing his job or acting in defiance of God's wishes for us to love one another?

In the end, he decided that it was his responsibility to God to play as hard as he could and make the best of the talents the Lord had given him. And that it's OK for the rest of us to do the same in our non-football endeavors, as long as we play by the rules and with an honest heart.

"I'm going to do the best that I can with every opportunity I get," Singletary says. "Sometimes it means walking away from something that appears to be very good. There are some things I don't want to win because the price is too high, and I have to know many years from now that I didn't compromise. That's the most important thing. When I go to bed at night, did I compromise today? Did I cheat anybody? Did I lie? Did I manipulate? It's like David said, 'Lord, search my heart and see if there is anything hidden in me, expose it, because I want to be right with You.'"

Singletary was referring to Psalm 139:23. The entire psalm reads:

> You have searched me, LORD,
>   and you know me.
> You know when I sit and when I rise;
>   you perceive my thoughts from afar.
> You discern my going out and my lying down;
>   you are familiar with all my ways.
> Before a word is on my tongue
>   you, LORD, know it completely.
> You hem me in behind and before,
>   and you lay your hand upon me.
> Such knowledge is too wonderful for me,
>   too lofty for me to attain.
>
> Where can I go from your Spirit?
>   Where can I flee from your presence?
> If I go up to the heavens, you are there;
>   if I make my bed in the depths, you are there.

If I rise on the wings of the dawn,
  if I settle on the far side of the sea,
even there your hand will guide me,
  your right hand will hold me fast.
If I say, "Surely the darkness will hide me
  and the light become night around me,"
even the darkness will not be dark to you;
  the night will shine like the day,
  for darkness is as light to you.

For you created my inmost being;
  you knit me together in my mother's womb.
I praise you because I am fearfully and wonderfully made;
  your works are wonderful,
  I know that full well.
My frame was not hidden from you
  when I was made in the secret place,
  when I was woven together in the depths of the earth.
Your eyes saw my unformed body;
  all the days ordained for me were written in your book
  before one of them came to be.
How precious to me are your thoughts, God!
  How vast is the sum of them!
Were I to count them,
  they would outnumber the grains of sand—
  when I awake, I am still with you.

If only you, God, would slay the wicked!
  Away from me, you who are bloodthirsty!
They speak of you with evil intent;
  your adversaries misuse your name.
Do I not hate those who hate you, LORD,
  and abhor those who are in rebellion against you?

I have nothing but hatred for them;
    I count them my enemies.
Search me, God, and know my heart;
    test me and know my anxious thoughts.
See if there is any offensive way in me,
    and lead me in the way everlasting.

"I want the Lord, not just that day when I have to stand in judgment," Singletary says. "But I want the Lord to be able to accept my prayers and say, 'Well done, son.' That's important to me."

Singletary isn't alone. Players like New York Giants Pro Bowl defensive end Justin Tuck, former Pro Bowl Denver Broncos offensive lineman Mark Schlereth, Washington Redskins safety Oshiomogho Atogwe, and others share the same religious goals and career aspirations. And it's just as violent a game today as it was twenty years ago.

Perhaps no one can attest to that as strongly as Schlereth, now an analyst for ESPN.

The former Idaho offensive lineman had seven surgeries before he got out of college. It was so bad, the school "retired" him after his junior season and would only let him back on the field his senior year after he begged. And even then, he had to sign a waiver releasing the school of any legal liability for the damage he was inflicting on his body.

The pro scouts took notice of his talent, but even though he had the size, quickness, and other physical attributes, his long list of injuries drove them away.

Instead of quitting, he cooked up a scheme with a teammate who was getting some looks. Marvin Washington, a defensive end for the University of Idaho, would call Schlereth whenever a scout would come to work him out, and Schlereth would show up and beg them to work him out too. The trickery was apparently successful because he was selected by the Washington Redskins in the tenth round of the 1989 draft. Schlereth worked his way into the starting lineup in no time, eventually earning two Pro Bowl invitations and playing in three Super Bowls: one with the Washington Redskins and two with the Denver Broncos.

Schlereth epitomized toughness and competitiveness for twelve NFL seasons. By the time he retired after the 2000 season, he'd undergone twenty-nine surgeries, including twenty on his knees.

"It's a violent game and people marvel at how I was able to play hurt. But this is what I was called to," says Schlereth, who hosted the Broncos Bible study at his home for six seasons.

It's hard not to laugh when Schlereth says he knew football was his calling. Most would have assumed it was a wrong number and hung up after the first seven surgeries. But the little voices in his head kept saying: *All's clear ahead.*

Schlereth's stories were legendary. One season, he developed a kidney stone and awoke writhing in pain the day before a Monday Night Football game against the Broncos' AFC West rival Oakland Raiders.

He waited for his wife to wake up at 7:00 a.m. to take him to the hospital where he spent most of the day on morphine and an IV drip waiting for the stone to pass. No luck.

At 9:30 p.m., doctors surgically removed the stone, and when Schlereth woke up the following morning, he needed morphine to staunch the pain of urinating. To the surprise of most everyone, Schlereth checked himself out of the hospital at 11:00 a.m., drove himself to the team's pregame meal, and started that night.

Another time, Schlereth was driven to practice after having an early-morning arthroscopic surgery to clean loose bodies out of the knee. He was sitting at his locker, bandages still wrapped around his knee, blood stains from where the incisions had been made hours earlier, when Pro Bowl wide receiver Rod Smith came strolling by on his way to the training room.

"Oh, shoot," Smith said, staring at Schlereth's knee.

"What?" said Schlereth.

"They gave me the day off [practice] because my hamstring is sore . . . You're going out there? [Long pause, heaves a deep breath out] OK, then I can't miss," he said.

Schlereth's tribulations were almost biblical. In the end, it was his unwillingness to quit and his resolve in the face of unending pain and adversity that earned him the respect of his teammates, coaches, and fans.

"There were times when I was incredibly disappointed and would pray to God and be like, 'Really? I have to have another surgery? Err, Lord, really? This is what You have for me right now?'" Schlereth says.

He's lived a blessed life, but there were moments when he felt a little like Job. Many are surprised to learn it wasn't a torn ligament or broken bone that nearly ended Schlereth's career.

He was stricken with Guillain-Barre syndrome—a disorder in which the body's immune system attacks its nerves, eventually causing paralysis—and missed most of the 1993 season after losing the feeling in his arms and legs. After so many surgeries, he must have thought the only things missing were the boils and perhaps a swarm of locusts. He was told that his career was over. Naturally, Schlereth ignored the doctors, prayed to the Lord, and rekindled his inner fire. When he showed up for training camp the following summer, it only made his legend grow.

Schlereth says his football celebrity gave him a voice and stature that allowed him to serve God's purpose in many ways.

"When I came to Denver and hosted a Bible study at my house, I saw a lot of men during that time give their life to Christ," he recalls. "I had a chance to minister to kids [after the shootings] at Columbine High School. I got to spend time with the victims and their families, and I was afforded the opportunity to hopefully bring comfort and to share the peace of Christ with them. I felt that's what I was being told to do."

It helped that he was 6-foot-3, 282 pounds and had a reputation for dealing with pain. When he reached out to love others in need, or to provide a shoulder to cry on, he was like a magnet, drawing people in to hear more. It's one of those ironies in life. When a big, powerful man acts big and powerful, he can seem brutish, distant, even feared. But when a powerful man is gentle and caring and loving, he becomes all the more powerful because he is loved back; he is admired for the control he has of that strength rather than feared for it.

Yet in the locker room where players are constantly looking for an advantage, he saw that his faith was sometimes perceived as a mark of weakness rather than a sign of strength. It's something you hear over and over from players of faith regardless of the generation in which they played.

What is it about people's perception of Christianity that makes it hard for them to understand that a man can lead a Bible study, love a grief-stricken kid, comfort an elderly neighbor, and still get up in an opponent's face on Sunday afternoon?

"For me," Schlereth shares, "it was important to be a child of Christ, but that doesn't mean I'm not one tough son of a gun. You know? Right? A lot of times there is this feeling of, 'Oh, there is the Bible-thumper of the team. Those guys are soft.' What? Because I try to love people and care for people, that makes me less of a football player? Not true.

"Go to the second chapter of Philippians where Paul is writing to the church of Philippi from prison and he's talking about how you should treat one another, how you should love one another, and be of the same mind, body, and spirit and treat others as more important than yourself. That was a big part of what I felt like I was doing."

Therefore if you have any encouragement from being united with Christ, if any comfort from his love, if any common sharing in the Spirit, if any tenderness and compassion, then make my joy complete by being like-minded, having the same love, being one in spirit and of one mind. Do nothing out of selfish ambition or vain conceit. Rather, in humility value others above yourselves, not looking to your own interests but each of you to the interests of others.

In your relationships with one another, have the same mind-set as Christ Jesus:

> *Who, being in very nature of God,*
> *did not consider equality with God something to be used to his own*
>   *advantage;*
> *rather, he made himself nothing*
> *by taking the very nature of a servant,*
> *being made in human likeness.*
> *And being found in appearance as a man,*
> *he humbled himself*
> *by becoming obedient to death—*
> *even death on a cross!*
> *Therefore God exalted him to the highest place*
> *and gave him the name that is above every name,*
> *that at the name of Jesus every knee should bow,*
> *in heaven and on earth and under the earth,*
> *and every tongue acknowledge that Jesus Christ is Lord,*
> *to the glory of God the Father.* (Philippians 2:1–11)

"That scripture still inspires me on a daily basis," Schlereth continues. "How am I loving people? Am I living out that particular scripture and regarding others as more important than myself? It was important to me to display that aspect of my life to the people around me including to my teammates."

GLADIATORS

Washington Redskins safety Oshiomogho Atogwe grew up in Windsor, Ontario, just across the river from Detroit. His father,

Aigbomoidi, who emigrated from Nigeria in 1974, worked at the Ford Motor Company as a mechanic and is retired. His mother, Babianna, still cleans rooms at a local hospital.

Atogwe's parents introduced their son to the concept of God as a child—the notion that there was a creator and protector, and that Oshiomogho (oh-SHIM-ago) would be held responsible for his actions. That was about the extent of his faith. He didn't go to church, he didn't know many people in his neighborhood who did, and his understanding of the Bible was limited to the Christmas story of the baby Jesus.

"The way I grew up, the norm was to play sports, run around chasing girls, hang out with friends, and you believed that was the way you were supposed to grow up," Atogwe explains. "You stayed out of trouble and didn't do anything against the law, but anything short of breaking the law was fine to do."

It wasn't until his freshman year at Stanford University, where he earned a degree in biological sciences and planned to enroll in medical school, that Oshiomogho became involved in the church.

There was a group that met monthly called Cardinal Life, which was basically a Christian athlete ministry for all the sports teams at Stanford. It was run by former NFL quarterback Steve Stenstrom and longtime Stanford religious counselor Jim Stump. Atogwe heard about the meetings from his Stanford teammates and committed his life to Christ in the spring semester of his freshman year.

"There were some older guys on the team who I looked up to that attended the meetings," Atogwe says. "I liked the way they carried themselves, their demeanor. They had something that was really different about them. It was a draw for me. And it changed my life drastically.

"I saw that there was another way to live my life. There were people saying that I wasn't supposed to be treating others or acting in the way that I was. Up to that point, I didn't know better. I just took it as, 'This is the way guys are supposed to be.' But then I saw there was a better way to live."

As Atogwe grew in his faith, he prospered on the field and was selected by the St. Louis Rams in the third round of the 2005 NFL draft. He quickly developed a reputation for consistency, intercepting 22 passes, forcing 16 fumbles, and amassing nearly 340 tackles in six seasons with the team.

In the summer of 2011, Atogwe had his best off-season ever. He signed a free agent contract with the Washington Redskins and married Jill Singletary, the daughter of former Bears linebacker Mike Singletary.

Two big goals in his life are to be the best husband he can be to his new bride and to be one of the hardest-hitting, most tenacious safeties the NFL has ever known.

Like Singletary and Schlereth, he is an example of a Christian who understands that he can be loving and caring and still compete at the highest level.

Atogwe says the time when he separates the loving husband from the aggressive, even violent, defender takes place in front of his locker. Perhaps like a lawyer standing quietly in a hallway before entering the courtroom to cross-examine a witness, or a surgeon scrubbing before entering the operating room, Atogwe also undergoes an emotional and physical metamorphosis where he leaves the troubles and distractions of the world behind and begins to focus on the man he must become and the task he must perform.

He says there is a "Gladiator/Spartacus" feel as he dresses in his armor, marches through the tunnel, and rushes the field to the sound of music, chanting, and sometimes smoke and fireworks.

"It's like you are going into battle," he says. "You put in your pads. You put on your pants. You pull on your shoulder pads, your cleats, and it's like you are armoring up. You are going to do battle against another team where the players are putting on their armor, too, and then you are going to meet in the middle of the arena to go at it. Praise God it's not for life and death."

Atogwe points out that while the game is violent, all the players on the field know the rules and agree to share the risks equally. As long as there is no malicious intent to harm one another, he believes the hardest of hits are OK in God's eyes. Most players share this belief.

Atogwe was once asked: If a receiver is looking the other way and you have him dead to rights, do you pull up and just make the tackle, or do you run through him even if the blow could cause him harm?

"You are going to lay him out," Atogwe replied quickly and without emotion. "As long as I'm playing by the rules I'm governed by, then God will be pleased by me. As long as I'm hitting them where I'm allowed to hit them, it's fair game. Everybody agreed to the rules. If he is hurt, you pray for him. He's in God's hands. You don't want to seriously harm anybody. I don't believe that is in the heart of a Christian. We are here to love each other and build them up. God wouldn't be OK with me trying to harm someone because we are putting the sport above the lives of the people He created. But He has called us to play this game 100 percent without fear or hesitation to His glory, and as long as we do that within the rules, I believe that in His eyes He is pleased with what we are doing."

New York Giants defensive captain and two-time Pro Bowl defensive end Justin Tuck shares Atogwe's beliefs, even during a year in which he was slowed by a series of injuries.

Tuck is a menace for quarterbacks. He's quick off the ball and bull-strong. He set Notre Dame's career sack record at 24.5 before graduating with a degree in management, and he had two quarterback sacks and three quarterback hurries to help lead the Giants to a 17–14 victory over the New England Patriots in Super Bowl XLII.

He got better with each successive season and seemed on the verge of establishing himself as one of the NFL's most dominant pass rushers after registering 11.5 sacks and being named to the Pro Bowl in 2010.

Then things fell apart.

In August 2011, the Giants were playing the New York Jets in their final preseason game. Late in the fourth quarter, the Jets ran a running play toward Tuck, who wasn't directly involved in the tackle. As the play came to a close, Tuck eased up, and that's when he got knocked over, creating a whiplash effect on his head. The incident caused inflammation, soreness, and muscle tension in his neck for weeks. It was a nagging injury that just wouldn't go away. And there were other nagging injuries too. At one point late in the 2011 season, Tuck was being treated by the team trainer for five different medical issues at the same time.

Tuck is a reminder that it's not just the offensive players who experience the pain and violence of the game. Careers are ended just as easily for the biggest and strongest defensive players on NFL Sundays.

So much is at stake for the player and his family, as evidenced by the series of events that take place when the player is being carted off the field and the television announcers tell us they are going to break for a commercial.

The team's doctors and trainers check the injury to see how quickly the player can be repaired and returned to the game.

The backup and his family quietly celebrate the unexpected opportunity to break into the lineup and show what he's got. (The wife shushes the kids in the stands, watching her husband's every move. "Come on, baby, do something big," she whispers, a few feet from the starter's wife.)

Agents for unemployed veterans still hoping for one more paycheck make plans to call the team for a workout.

Practice-squad players hope they'll get moved up to the fifty-three-man roster.

The general manager wants the injured star back on the field, but he also knows the injury will affect the player's value in the next contract negotiation. He's got leverage.

The injured player and his family are concerned about his health and how it could affect his career. They watch as his teammates pat the replacement on the butt in encouragement.

The vultures are circling.

"You come in and work out all off-season and set yourself up to have another great year, and then you get hurt. I don't think it was intentional. It happens. So how do you look at that?" Tuck asks.

As former Vikings coach Brad Childress says in chapter 1, "faith guys" believe that the injury is part of God's plan for their lives and expect something good to come out of it. What else is there to do, but treat the injury, endure the pain of rehabilitation, and return as quickly as possible? Having a good attitude and an understanding that God has something special in store for you is half the battle.

"I realize that you really don't have a testimony if you don't have some test," Tuck says. "Just because you are a Christian doesn't mean you are always going to have sunny days and the sky is always going to be blue."

Tuck harkens back to Job's trials in the Bible and says that it's the difficult times that make our faith grow. That's when we realize God hasn't left us.

"A lot of people like to say, 'Where is your God now?'" continues Tuck. "But He hasn't left me. You know He's teaching me something right now. What that is, hasn't been revealed to me yet. But you just have to be patient and keep doing what you can do. Me complaining about it isn't going to help the situation. You go get your treatment, do your work, and continue to go."

Tuck is convinced God has a unique plan for each of us, regardless of our career choice, wealth, looks, or social standing. And while it might seem that He's given some of us a greater share of these gifts, we must have faith that it is part of His plan.

One of Tuck's favorite passages is the parable in Matthew 25:14–30:

It will be like a man going on a journey, who called his servants and entrusted his wealth to them. To one he gave five bags of gold, to another two bags, and to another one bag, each according to his ability. Then he went on his journey. The man who had received five bags of gold went at once and put his money to work and gained five bags more. So also, the one with two bags of gold gained two more. But the man who had received one bag went off, dug a hole in the ground and hid his master's money.

After a long time the master of those servants returned and settled accounts with them. The man who had received five bags of gold brought the other five. "Master," he said, "you entrusted me with five bags of gold. See, I have gained five more."

His master replied, "Well done, good and faithful servant! You have been faithful with a few things; I will put you in charge of many things. Come and share your master's happiness!"

The man with two bags of gold also came. "Master," he said, "you entrusted me with two bags of gold; see, I have gained two more."

His master replied, "Well done, good and faithful servant! You have been faithful with a few things; I will put you in charge of many things. Come and share your master's happiness!"

Then the man who had received one bag of gold came. "Master," he said, "I knew that you are a hard man, harvesting where you have not sown and gathering where you have not scattered seed. So I was afraid and went out and hid your gold in the ground. See, here is what belongs to you."

His master replied, "You wicked, lazy servant! So you knew that I harvest where I have not sown and gather where I have not scattered seed? Well then, you should have put my money on deposit with the bankers, so that when I returned I would have received it back with interest.

"So take the bag of gold from him and give it to the one who has

ten bags. For whoever has will be given more, and they will have an abundance. Whoever does not have, even what they have will be taken from them. And throw that worthless servant outside, into the darkness, where there will be weeping and gnashing of teeth."

"He's saying that we should do the best we can with the gifts we are given," Tuck explains. "Whether you are a lawyer, a football player, or an author. Whenever you have a talent, you are required to maximize it."

Like Singletary, Schlereth, Atogwe, and thousands of other current and former Christian football players, Tuck has also come to the conclusion that as violent as the game might be, God calls on us to play as hard as we can. Anything less would dishonor the Lord and the gifts He has bestowed upon us—whether they be athletic abilities, a musical ear, mathematical genius, or a sculptor's imagination.

"I don't think He wants us to pull up. You can be dominant and be humble about it," Tuck says. "You are able to be dominant in your field because God has given you that grace and allowed you to step into those avenues where perhaps other people can't. You have an obligation to give it your all."

WHAT MAKES YOU UNIQUE?

God-given talent. What is that talent for each of us? Is it to sell or negotiate or build? Is it to nurture or cure or treat? Mike Singletary isn't going to cure cancer. He's not going to uncover a secret fuel source. He's not going to design an underwater city.

Football is Singletary's gift. Sure, he could be successful in other professions, but this is clearly the one he was designed for. Singletary, who later went on to coach the San Francisco 49ers and is now an assistant coach for the Minnesota Vikings, was fifty-three at the start of the 2011 NFL season.

His neck is still thick, his shoulders wide and powerful. The intensity is still there in his eyes and in his heart. A man thirty years younger and a head taller would be ill-advised to challenge Mike Singletary today. These athletes truly are different. We pay good money to see them in their prime, but they are still athletes very late into their lives. What they do with the fame those abilities permit them is up to them. For some, it's just about playing a game. For others, it's a platform to be used to bring attention to Christ.

"What it came down to," he says, "is that this is my gift. And the Lord is more concerned with my heart. The Lord is concerned more about my intent and why I am doing what I am doing. I didn't want to hurt anybody. I was playing the game as hard as I could play it to honor Him."

More than any other team sport, football is a game where the players put their health and livelihood on the line each time they take the field. The players have a tremendous respect for one another because they understand that. "I am out here in my armor, ready to go to war. Who knows if I will be able to walk off the field? Who knows if I am walking on it for the last time?" Singletary points out.

"People say, 'How can you be a Christian and go out there and play such a violent sport?' I would say, 'How can you go out there and play such a violent sport and *not* be a man of faith?'

"One of the greatest things I had going for me as a player is that every time I walked on the field I always knew that God was with me."

Singletary retired after the 1992 season. Within his twelve NFL seasons, he went to the Pro Bowl ten consecutive times and was inducted into the Hall of Fame in 1998.

The image most fans outside Chicago have of Mike Singletary came from the lens of the television camera. It loved him. He would squat and lean forward, ready to drive runners backward. And his eyes, focused intently on the quarterback, were wide and large. On cold Chicago days, when his breath turned to vapor, he was a made-for-TV star.

Singletary says that was just a side effect of a growing media, hungry for tough characters they could promote for their Sunday matinee. In his heart and mind, every snap of the ball was an opportunity to praise the Lord.

"I always said, 'Lord, every play I'm going to give You everything I have. From the bottom of my feet all the way to the top of my head, I'm going to give everything I've got, every tackle, every block.' If the ball was thrown a hundred yards away, I was going to run as hard as I could run to get there," he says. "I thought about one thing, and that's giving God what Jesus Christ gave for me on the cross—and that's everything. That's how I was going to play. And I was at peace with that."

CHRISTIAN LEADERSHIP

Singletary was a player who led by example on and off the field. A father of seven, he was a Pro Bowl player who didn't play the field or party or gamble, and he didn't associate with those who did.

He was a leader who commanded the respect of his teammates first and foremost because he was a tenacious, fearless, unrelenting linebacker who was, above all, successful at his craft.

And that gave him a voice off the field, to speak and be heard about the Word of God. So it's fair to ask: Would Singletary have been the Christian example that he was to his teammates had he been a benchwarmer? Or was it the mastery of his craft that gave him a voice to share the Word?

The same question holds for corporate America, where it's often said that companies are a reflection of the man or woman at the top.

If the CEO is a risk-taking swashbuckler, a real playboy who made a fortune with borrowed money, his junior executives are more likely to emulate the great success of their leader and adopt a "go for broke" approach to business. No risk, no reward, right? Look what it did for the boss.

If the CEO is a conservative leader, who goes to great lengths to eliminate risk, and is willing to accept a smaller return if it ensures the safety of the company's investment . . . well, his charges probably know the fastest way to the executive washroom will require a different path. No reason to be foolish and risk the house, right? Look what it did for the boss.

But regardless which CEO is yours, it's unlikely that you'll seek out the advice of the mail room clerk, the loading dock manager, or the night watchman. If that's the highest he has climbed the corporate ladder, he must not be very wise.

Matt Hasselbeck came to understand this when he was selected by the Green Bay Packers in the sixth round of the 1998 NFL draft out of Boston College. That season he was cut and re-signed to the practice squad, where he could watch and learn from Pro Bowl quarterback Brett Favre and backup Doug Pederson.

The Packers had one of the most religious teams in the NFL at the time, but also one of its toughest. They were coming off back-to-back Super Bowl appearances with a 35–21 victory over the New England Patriots in Super Bowl XXXI and a 31–24 loss to the Denver Broncos in Super Bowl XXXII. And the locker room was jam-packed with genuine Christians like defensive lineman Reggie White, wide receiver Robert Brooks, and kicker Ryan Longwell.

"They were strong Christian guys who were consistent about their faith, and everyone would hang on every word they said because they were so good at their jobs," Hasselbeck recalls. "They had instant respect, and that really opened my eyes to things."

These same guys were the first to invite players over to their homes for dinner or to hang out. Friendships with Christian teammates were easy to come by. And Bible study was well attended.

Hasselbeck said that aside from his father—Don Hasselbeck, a former tight end for the New England Patriots, Minnesota Vikings, New York Giants, and Los Angeles Raiders during a nine-year NFL career—he hadn't been around many Christians who were really good, hard-nosed football players. In fact, most Christian players at the time had a bad reputation.

"A lot of times in the locker room, you'd hear players or coaches say, 'Oh, he's a Christian.' What they meant is that the player was soft. That used to really bother me because I never ever, ever wanted to be soft or wimpy."

In Green Bay, Hasselbeck saw that the notion of a soft Christian was a misnomer. Overnight, he had role models who showed him that a Christian can be competitive—going for the jugular if you will—yet still love their opponents when the whistle blew.

"I see these guys that are bad dudes, like Reggie White and [offensive lineman] Adam Timmerman, and I mean they are *really* bad dudes. They are just blowing people up. They are the best in the world at what they do, and yet, they are the nicest guys and great Christians.

"You'd see Reggie knock a guy on his back, totally break his spirit, and then reach out a hand to help him up off the ground. Adam Timmerman was the same way. He had a little nasty streak to him on the field. He's what you'd call a real man's man. But on his off day, he'd be hunting or building something in his garage. We had guys like that every year."

The image of the "weak" or "soft" Christian had been around for years. And although players like Singletary and Reggie White did their best to dispel the notion, it took a while for players and coaches to accept the idea that Christians could be as vicious as the next guy. And . . . that it was OK.

"BIBLE BANGERS"

When the Philadelphia Eagles hired Andy Reid in January 1999, the team was lousy. It had finished 3-13 the previous year and hadn't had a winning season in three years. What's worse, the players had a reputation for being pushovers.

"When I started this job," Reid shares, "this team was known as a soft football team of 'Bible Bangers.' That was what I was told. Literally. 'Bible Bangers.' So in my first meeting with the players, I said, 'Listen, I went to a religious institution. I played with returning missionaries who had tremendous faith. But when we went to play the game, we played at 110 miles an hour and it was like, "We are going to rip your head off." That's how we roll.'"

Reid, an offensive lineman at Brigham Young University, studies the Scriptures each morning, attends Bible study, and makes a pastor available to his players. Like Singletary, he thinks if Jesus lived on earth today, He'd be the sort of person who would go all out.

"I firmly believe if Christ came back today and decided He wanted to play this game, He'd be our middle linebacker. He'd be the toughest guy on the field. So I don't buy that 'Bible Banger' image. I told them, 'You guys keep studying the Scriptures and doing your thing. I'm not changing that. I'm encouraging you to do it. But that doesn't take away from your toughness on the football field. In fact, it should carry over to the football field.'"

The Eagles would eventually become known as one of the most aggressive, punch-you-in-the-nose teams in the NFL. Former defensive coordinator Jim Johnson, who passed away from skin cancer in 2009, was the architect of the defense, and the Eagles were known for blitzing, stunting, attacking defenses. But it didn't happen all at once, and Reid, like most employees who are new to a job and want to make a big splash, suffered during the early setbacks and learning curve.

"I remember my first year," he says. "We were getting destroyed.

We were terrible, absolutely terrible. And I remember sitting there thinking through it, and I'm normally very optimistic. But I was feeling sorry for myself, and I was sitting there in the bottom of the Vet, the basement man, in this tiny little office, with beer dripping down the side of the walls [from the tap rooms above], and it's got to be one o'clock in the morning, and I'm pouting and feeling sorry for myself and then it hits me. 'You are a big sissy. Here is Christ, who sat there in the Garden of Gethsemane, bleeding from every pore, and you are sitting here moaning about football games and fans and all these things you have racing through your head. You have to get off your butt and you gotta roll, man. You gotta go and not worry about all that stuff.'"

That's how Andy Reid tries to live his life whether he's fighting through a bad season or lending support to a family member. But as strong as his own faith is, he says there is a terrible risk to pushing his own beliefs on others.

"I think there are certain things that have caused wars and strife throughout history," Reid admits. "Money, religion, and women are three prominent ones, and politics probably fits in there somewhere too. So I told the team, 'I don't want players preaching their beliefs to other players unless they are asked. We are together for too many hours. If somebody comes to you and wants to talk, that's cool— share your faith, but I don't want any arguments over it.'

"I've said before that a lot of the things you go through in life, and how you pull through them, come down to what sort of foundation you've built and that you can fall back on. Our faith is that foundation, and it dictates a lot about how we've handled things both in the good times and the bad. Is life going to be perfect? No. Is football going to be perfect? No. Is your faith going to be perfect? Well, the heavenly Father's plan is perfect, but we've all got our weaknesses trying to follow that plan. So you need something to fall back on, a structure in your life with some rules and guidance. That's why I think it's great for players to be exposed to faith through their peers, as long as it's not forced on them. Not everyone is a believer."

Reid sticks to his guns on that. While former Indianapolis coach Tony Dungy and former Minnesota Vikings coach Brad Childress talked to their players about God in the locker room, Reid says he won't do that. He sees to it that team chaplain Herb Lusk holds a Bible study every Thursday and there is a chapel service the morning of the game. No wives, no families, just the team.

He says that his own prayers are kept short and that he never prays to win. "I have a feeling God probably looks at both teams," he says with a chuckle. "And He probably has some bigger issues than whether the Eagles win Sunday." Instead, Reid prays that God gives him the guidance to make the right decisions, that the minds of his assistants stay clear and strong, that the players avoid injury, and that everyone performs to the best of his God-given ability. "Boom," he says. "That's it. Go play."

Reid's approach to many things in life is short and crisp. He's personable, but there's not a lot of wasted chitchat. He believes in structure, planning, practice, execution, and ultimately he believes there is a God in heaven who has a plan for us. And while Reid might get frustrated and disappointed in himself and others, there is no going back in life. He worries only about the "now." So no matter where he finds himself, he develops a plan, pushes aside his personal fears, and attacks. He believes that this philosophy originates from his faith and that the best way to lead his team, his family, and his community is to let them see him living that faith every day.

"The heavenly Father has given me an opportunity to be here, and what an opportunity it is. One out of thirty-two guys in the world has the opportunity He has given me, and I'm going to take advantage of it. I love it and I give it everything I have every day and I let the chips fall where they may.

"In all parts of your life, you are going to be given obstacles. Our earth life is just a trial so we can return to the heavenly Father. The question is how you as an individual are going to sort that out. Everyone does it a little different. I'm going to attack. I'm coming at it. If it's a problem, I'm attacking the problem. I don't sit here and fear anything. That's not what I do."

3

FAMILY SACRIFICES

While he was still speaking, a bright cloud covered them, and a voice from the cloud said, "This is my Son, whom I love; with him I am well pleased. Listen to him!"

—Matthew 17:5

It's a Thursday morning in late September when a group of Arizona Cardinals wives gather by the pool at offensive tackle Levi Brown's home for their weekly Bible study. Kicker Jay Feely's wife, Rebecca, has made her famous scrambled eggs. And Lynette Brown, the hostess, ordered coffee, cinnamon rolls, and muffins from a nearby Paradise Bakery. Dreama Graves, the wife of Cardinals general manager Rod Graves, is leading the study, and as wives stroll in a few minutes before 10:00 a.m., it dawns on her that at forty-three, she's closer to the age of the wives' mothers than their girlfriends.

This Cardinals gathering isn't unique. All throughout the NFL, teams hold Bible studies for wives and girlfriends, separate studies for couples, and sometimes a third study just for the players.

It's the women, though, who form some of the most extraordinary bonds during these spiritual gatherings.

While their lives may appear glamorous, even privileged when their pictures appear in the paper or when they attend a social event outfitted in diamonds and the latest fashions, that's hardly the reality of the life of an NFL wife.

Many are forced to give up promising careers and small businesses to follow their husbands from one city to the next. When they are not packing the house or pulling their kids out of school, they are nursing their husbands' broken bodies and helping them rebuild their bruised egos. They struggle with self-identity issues, grapple with the insecurities of nonguaranteed contracts, and take calls from family members seeking financial support, as well as friends asking for game tickets. And oh, don't bring up the groupies, the ones who linger at every training camp, team hotel, restaurant, wine bar, and ice-cream parlor.

It's at these Bible studies where the wives and girlfriends can let their hair down, share their problems with women in similar circumstances, and seek the spiritual and emotional support they need to keep their children and their marriages on the right path.

Graves chose a book titled *He Speaks to Me: Preparing to Hear the Voice of God* by Priscilla Shirer as the text for this year's wives' Bible study. It's about opening yourself up to God so you can hear Him speak to you. The group was instructed to read two chapters before their meeting and to be prepared to share their insights into what it means to hear God.

This particular week, Dreama's group is focusing on scripture in 1 Samuel 3 about a young boy who hears God speaking to him. Children face many unknowns in their lives and can be manipulated because of their innocence, but it also gives them certain advantages. Rather than just ignoring the voice in their heads, they freely explore it without judgment or cynicism. What child says to herself, "Ah, that's crazy. I'm hearing voices"? Instead, children start walking toward the sound to discover the source. The takeaway from the wives' conversation was that we should have a childlike relationship with God that allows us to be open to what He is saying to us.

The boy Samuel ministered before the LORD *under Eli. In those days the word of the* LORD *was rare; there were not many visions.*

One night Eli, whose eyes were becoming so weak that he could barely see, was lying down in his usual place. The lamp of God had not yet gone out, and Samuel was lying down in the house of the LORD, *where the ark of God was. Then the* LORD *called Samuel.*

Samuel answered, "Here I am." And he ran to Eli and said, "Here I am; you called me."

But Eli said, "I did not call; go back and lie down." So he went and lay down.

Again the LORD *called, "Samuel!" And Samuel got up and went to Eli and said, "Here I am; you called me."*

"My son," Eli said, "I did not call; go back and lie down."

Now Samuel did not yet know the LORD: *The word of the* LORD *had not yet been revealed to him.*

A third time the LORD *called, "Samuel!" And Samuel got up and went to Eli and said, "Here I am; you called me."*

Then Eli realized that the LORD *was calling the boy. So Eli told Samuel, "Go and lie down, and if he calls you, say, 'Speak,* LORD, *for your servant is listening.'" So Samuel went and lay down in his place.*

The LORD *came and stood there, calling as at the other times, "Samuel! Samuel!"*

Then Samuel said, "Speak, for your servant is listening."

And the LORD *said to Samuel: "See, I am about to do something in Israel that will make the ears of everyone who hears about it tingle. At that time I will carry out against Eli everything I spoke against his family—from beginning to end. For I told him that I would judge his family forever because of the sin he knew about; his sons blasphemed God, and he failed to restrain them. Therefore I swore to the house of*

Eli, 'The guilt of Eli's house will never be atoned for by sacrifice or offering.'"

Samuel lay down until morning and then opened the doors of the house of the Lord. He was afraid to tell Eli the vision, but Eli called him and said, "Samuel, my son."

Samuel answered, "Here I am."

"What was it he said to you?" Eli asked. "Do not hide it from me. May God deal with you, be it ever so severely, if you hide from me anything he told you." So Samuel told him everything, hiding nothing from him. Then Eli said, "He is the Lord; let him do what is good in his eyes."

The Lord was with Samuel as he grew up, and he let none of Samuel's words fall to the ground. And all Israel from Dan to Beersheba recognized that Samuel was attested as a prophet of the Lord. The Lord continued to appear at Shiloh, and there he revealed himself to Samuel through his word. (1 Samuel 3)

Graves, who tries to keep the study to ninety minutes because some of the wives have children in school for half a day, asks the group what it thought of the passage and what each of the wives was doing to hear God in her own life.

Rebecca Feely, the mother of three girls aged three to ten and an eight-year-old boy, was a pre-med major at the University of Michigan before dropping out to pursue a modeling career in Chicago. "It was a meat market," she said about her time in the city. She returned to Ann Arbor to finish her degree in kinesiology and was applying to medical school when she met Jay, the Wolverines' kicker, who would sign a free agent contract with the Atlanta Falcons two years later. At thirty-five, she is one of the elder stateswomen in the group and also one of its most devout Christians.

"There is a spiritual dynamic in every situation we encounter, and we need to be able to discern that," she says in response to Graves's question. "God has a purpose and plan for all the good and bad that we are going through. Football, our careers, that's not God in our lives. That's just a job that can be used for a greater good that impacts others. Or we can use it selfishly and let it draw us away from God to make bad choices. We need to be open to hearing from Him."

The study has come at a good time for Rebecca, who is going through a difficult time in her personal life. Her parents, Jack and Edie Dawson, are staying at their daughter's home because Jack had been diagnosed with bladder cancer and needed surgery in Phoenix. There were complications when a blocked kidney became infected. Then, just after Rebecca had left Bible study the previous Thursday, her father developed sepsis, went into shock, and nearly died. Rebecca had spent two days going back and forth from home to the intensive care unit and was exhausted from the emotional drain when her mind turned to what she was learning in Bible study.

"I was like, 'OK, God. What are You trying to accomplish in this? I need to hear something from You to help me discern why our family is going through this,'" Feely says.

There is never a good time for a family member to fall ill. While fans have this image of professional athletes as healthy, famous, and rich, personal tragedies often go unnoticed. The Cardinals started the 2011 season 1-3, and Jay Feely, who was sharing his wife's pain, converted just three out of six field goals.

Rebecca was looking after the kids, keeping the house together, and rushing back and forth to the hospital. The stress was building up as concerned family members waited and prayed for good news. In recent years, walls had been built between Rebecca's siblings and their parents, and Rebecca and her mother. There had been disagreements over the years that were never resolved. But her dad's near death experience shattered those walls as each family member realized "we could actually lose him." Rebecca and her mother brought up subjects that had been buried for years and began working through them.

Rebecca was her mother's sixth child, her father's third, and the only child between them. Her older sister Pam died of a brain aneurysm at the age of eighteen when Rebecca was two. Her twenty-four-year-old brother Steve was murdered in Texas when she was seven. And her sister Roberta died after being born prematurely. "There was a lot of dysfunction. I found God in college and was able to heal from a lot of the trauma," she said.

Now that her dad was gravely ill, "Mom and I were able to work things out that we never would have brought up had he not been that sick," Feely says. "I shared this with the girls. You might look at every situation you are going through and ask, 'Why me?' But when you allow yourself to step away from that situation and see there is a greater purpose, and when you find that purpose, it becomes a beautiful thing and a stepping-stone to a closer walk with Him."

Rebecca's story opens up the group emotionally. One at a time, they begin sharing their stories. One player's wife says her father-in-law has been diagnosed with cancer, and it is affecting their family too. Another wife admits to having a hard time fitting in with her new community after her husband was traded. A third speaks of financial struggles. "I know how it is to feel lost and wonder, 'Why are we here? Why do I feel so alone? What's the purpose in it?' But you have to listen to God," Feely says, reemphasizing the day's Bible study lesson.

KIDS, SPOUSES, STRESS

Feely's sick father serves as a reminder that the rich and famous aren't any different from the rest of us, at least not in God's eyes. For most NFL chaplains, Bible studies are an important opportunity to reach players on a personal level and help them get through some of the most challenging moments in their lives. It has nothing to do with catching a deep pass or getting around a three-hundred-pound blocker. That's kid stuff. That's the part of the players' lives they are most confident and knowledgable about. Now, getting a baby to sleep because daddy has practice in the morning, or being confronted by a two-year-old who says no to everything, or getting your wife to see it your way—that's more of a challenge. NFL marriages undergo the same trials as those of any other couple, no matter the size of the house or the bank account. And their kids may be well dressed, but that doesn't mean they don't throw the same tantrums like everyone else's child. This is why Bible studies can play an important role in the growth of the player, not just spiritually, but in everyday, practical ways.

The purpose of Bible study is to receive spiritual education and enlightenment, but team pastors provide services well beyond that. Their job is to serve the needs of their players in the same way they tend to the needs of their congregation at church. This group is young, well-known, and rich by most standards. But the players and their wives are also inexperienced, usually far from home and in need of someone they can trust with private matters. Most come from communities where the notion of hiring a psychologist, marriage counselor, or child development expert is humorous. That's the preacher's job.

In 2011, Brett Fuller entered his ninth season as the Washington Redskins' chaplain. He was one of the founding members of Grace Covenant Church in Chantilly, Virginia, when it started in 1982 with twelve worshipers meeting in church basements, high schools, hotels, and community centers. Today, they have their own building and need five weekend services to cater to their 2,500 parishioners, including retired Redskins greats Darrell Green, Art Monk, Charles Mann, and Ken Harvey.

A naturally gifted speaker, Fuller uses Bible study to introduce subjects like: How to be a good husband or wife. What expectations can you have of your spouse? What does it mean to "train" your children?

Child rearing is one of the most popular topics at his couples Bible study, given the age of his audience. Most families are just starting out and are dealing with toddlers, though a few have older children. In most cases, there is still time to influence their children's lives, and Pastor Fuller and his wife, Cynthia, parents of seven children, spend hours answering questions from young NFL parents.

One subject he spends a lot of time addressing is the difference between *raising* children and *training* them, he says. Remember, these are the children of wealthy celebrities. That comes with a whole set of social advantages and entitlement expectations that most parents don't face.

"There are a lot of people who raise their children and believe they just need to provide an umbrella of safety so nothing harms them; to nurture them with love and provide for them with food, clothing, shelter, and education," Fuller tells the couples. "But they don't train their children to be the kind of people they want them to be when they get older. In other words, they don't work on character development. They don't teach them how to share when they are young or how to restrain their desires.

"What does it mean to say no to something you really want, in deference to something you really need? Parents ought to be involved in the training of their children. We're not talking about manipulating them so the children become what the parents want. We're talking about getting down on the inside of their souls, spending quality time on a regular basis so the parents can mold who they are supposed to be in God's way," he says.

There is no instruction manual on raising a child. Fortunately NFL couples can ask the pastor and his wife questions without the second-guessing that comes from asking for advice from a parent, sibling, or close friend.

TRUST, SEX, AND MARRIAGE

Chaplains say another popular Bible study focuses on how to build better relationships and marriages. Just as many NFL couples are new to parenthood, so, too, are they new to marriage. In 2010, the average age of an NFL player was just 26.4 years, and wives are usually a few years younger.

In the early years, marriage isn't that unlike two single people living together. Both parties still think about their own needs and desires first. Arguments are to be won, without regard to the impact it will have on the spouse who suffered the defeat. And huge arguments can be overshadowed by great sex that only serves to obscure and delay the uncomfortable discussion that needs to take place.

"Every couple comes into a marriage with expectations about what the other party ought to be for them, and generally speaking, when that doesn't happen, the 'love' they had diminishes," Fuller tells the players and their wives. "It never happens consciously. But that is when we begin to define love. Love doesn't have anything to do with feelings. It has everything to do with the decisions we make. Rather than come into a relationship based on what the other party can do for me, I have to decide that the other party is not supposed to be anything for me. I am supposed to be something for them," Fuller says. "As soon as I expect them to be what I need them to be, then I am almost demanding that they become that. And if they are not, then I am going to become disappointed in them, disillusioned, and generally more distant.

"So rather than have an expectation," he continues, "choose right now to concentrate on yourself. What do I need to be for them? It's not 50-50 any longer; it's 100-100. I give 100 percent to them, and they give 100 percent to me. I don't expect anything from them, and they don't expect anything from me. Now, is that hard to do? Yes. Almost impossible. But when we make an effort to do so, we are less disappointed and are always focusing on ourselves when something has gone wrong rather than blaming them."

Of course, NFL players don't have ordinary relationships. And that's something most men, but especially their wives, are unhappy to discover, Fuller observes.

"Wow, these wives have no idea what they are getting into when they marry a ballplayer," Fuller shares. "The ballplayer can provide in unusual ways and that's great. And they love that, and it's beautiful. I'm glad. And the wives usually genuinely love the man. But when they marry him, they forget that everybody else thinks they have a piece of him too. So when they show up at an event together, the wife will barely be noticed. Hardly anybody says, 'And you? Your name?' They only want to meet him. So the wife is often ignored, and being ignored is hard to become comfortable with.

"So the expectations the NFL wife must have of her husband are: 'Sweetheart, are you going to make sure I'm introduced? Are you going to make sure I'm right there with you, and I'm treated well and respected everywhere I go?' The husband does the best he can, but sometimes he forgets and sometimes he's so inundated that he can't. And that's when she has to be understanding and forgiving. And that's not always easy either."

Most women can deal with being a little ignored as long as they get the one-on-one time they need with their husbands later. But that's not the part that creates the biggest worries and insecurities . . . it's the other women.

Imagine your husband, an accountant for ACME Inc., is really good-looking and has such a great body that even your best friends tease you about it. And imagine he travels for weeks at a time on business and another ten weekends a year to an accountant camp, where you know for a fact that there are accountant groupies. Yeah, I know, a little far-fetched, but . . . and the accountant groupies are usually eighteen to twenty-four years old and very aggressive. How would that make you feel sitting at home dealing with a child going through the terrible twos?

"There is a lot of travel and the woman has to understand that not only do people want the personality, but there are women out there pulling on this guy and he has to be nice without being attentive and that's a hard balance," Fuller says. "He can't misrepresent the organization by ignoring them, but he can't violate the relationship with his wife by being too interested."

Fuller ministers the players on setting boundaries. As a group, they create a list of things players should and shouldn't do in the way they treat and interact with other women.

"He shouldn't receive communications from different ladies via text messages," Fuller cautions. "His wife can take his cell phone and look at his messages, and even if it's innocent, how will that make her feel? It will create doubt.

"He should not talk to women outside of business. Sometimes a player will go to a luncheon. Even if his agent employs female lawyers that will accompany him, he should only meet that person at a public place—not the team hotel before a game.

"We say to the players, 'Listen, this is what you've got to do. You want trust? You want confidence in your relationship so every time you come home your wife doesn't have to question where you were or why you were ten minutes late or who that woman was on your text or ask to see your cell so she knows who called you today? If you want the kind of confidence where those questions are not an issue, then you have to keep these boundaries.'"

Fuller acknowledges it's hard for the players because they feel that they are being accused of something horrible when they've done nothing wrong. They feel that their wives or girlfriends are restricting them from living freely. It can lead to resentment. But Fuller is clear that the responsibility falls on the player because he is traveling away from home and is often being chased by women. He encourages each player to ask himself: *How must it feel from the other side where my wife is sitting at home?*

"Once they make these changes, in my experience," Fuller says, "they like it when they come home and their wives trust them and all the tension disappears."

GOD SPEAKS

Back in Arizona, the wives have been laughing and sharing for an hour when Graves asks the group what other issues are affecting their lives. The wives come from all walks of life. Some are from the inner city, while others are from the countryside. Some are barely out of college, while others have attended their children's high school graduations. More important, some are new to Christ or returning after a long absence, while others have been on their walk for many years. What bind them are their desire to know God, their growing friendship, and the fears and insecurities that come with being an NFL wife.

Cabrina Womack has been married to her husband, Cardinals offensive lineman Floyd Womack, for three years. She met him at a nail salon, which usually gets a few laughs. Floyd is 6-foot-4, 328 pounds and was the biggest man in the building, she says. As she signed in at the front desk, she looked him over from head to toe, and he just took her breath away. "It was love at first sight," she shares.

Cabrina grew up in Hattiesburg, Mississippi, across the street from her family church, which she attended mostly for the friendships. When Cabrina became pregnant at sixteen, her mother decided to start a new career in Jackson, Mississippi, about ninety miles north, packed her bags, and left. Cabrina was left alone to raise her baby and finish school. Her parents were divorced, and she would take her father's child support check, buy groceries, pay the electric bill, and "do whatever needed to be done.

"When Mom left me, there was a lot of emptiness, and it was

like I was backed into a corner," Cabrina says. "It felt like I had no one. The only thing I felt could help me was God. And once I took it serious and started to build a relationship with Him, I was like, 'Wow, all that time I was hurting and going through all this pain, the answer was right there.' From that point on, I took my faith very seriously and I just knew that God was my provider, and I didn't have to look to my mom and my dad and my grandmother and my friends and my family. I always went to Him first."

She moved to Jackson a year later to attend Jackson State. Her mother remarried in 2003, and her stepfather, Dr. Steven Hayne, a pathologist for the state of Mississippi, offered Cabrina a job at the morgue. She quit college and began working with him on autopsies: taking photos, typing up reports, labeling toxicology. It could run well past 1:00 or 2:00 a.m. She'd been working there four years when she met Floyd, and a year later he asked her to move with him to Seattle where he was playing for the Seahawks.

During the wives Bible study, Cabrina tells the women that she was confident she wasn't turning a deaf ear to God. She has been through so much, she says, that when God is trying to get her attention, she's sure she hears Him. And when things start going wrong for her and Floyd, they take a step back and try and evaluate what the Lord is saying.

"When I have a serious feeling about something that's on my heart, I know that's God speaking to me," she says. "Any little feeling, any little thing on my heart, I don't take it lightly."

Floyd has had trouble with nagging injuries throughout his career. He was selected by the Seattle Seahawks in the fourth round of the 2001 draft. At the beginning of the 2011 season, he injured his shoulder during training camp and went on injured reserve, sidelining him for the entire season. At thirty-two, it could be the end of an eleven-year career.

"Floyd will tell you when he's not giving God the time he should,"

Cabrina says. "[God] uses football to bring him closer. Injuries. I told Floyd, God is trying to get your attention and you need to listen and you need to pray and ask God, 'What do I need to do?'"

Cabrina is thankful for the team Bible study because it keeps her connected to her faith during the season when she is away from her home church. She says each meeting teaches her something new about what God expects out of her as a woman, a wife, a mom, and a friend. "Sometimes it's about being patient or being trustworthy or being a good friend or a supportive wife. That's why I attend Bible study. It's a place to meet women like myself, where I can learn and grow. It's an important part of my life."

MODEL BUSINESSWOMAN

Though Bible study is a great place to share and learn from one another, it's not the only place NFL wives get an education. Some women of faith develop relationships at a local church, away from the team. Or they and their husbands simply get together with like-minded team-mates and their wives every other week over dinner or an evening out. This is where NFL wives and families have a chance to learn about the pitfalls of the NFL from those veterans and their wives who are will-ing to look out for the newbies and transplants.

Octavia McDougle, vice president of the NFL Players' Wives Association, a nonprofit group of current and former wives whose goal is to raise funds for charitable organizations, has participated in NFL union-sponsored business classes in recent years. She's an example of a savvy businesswoman who saw early in her husband's career that she needed to prepare for a life after football.

Octavia met Stockar McDougle when they were both freshmen at Deerfield Beach High School in Deerfield Beach, Florida. He was her first boyfriend. The couple married after high school graduation, and then he left for the University of Oklahoma where he'd earned a football scholarship. The couple had their first child a year later and maintained a long-distance relationship with Octavia making frequent trips from her home in Florida.

Octavia started a hair salon with her mother called Beauty Explosion and used the profits to support the family. This independence gave Octavia a degree of motivation and self-confidence that's rare at such a young age. It was a life skill that she wouldn't relinquish easily.

McDougle, a 6-foot-6, 335-pound offensive lineman, was selected by the Detroit Lions in the first round of the 2000 draft. The family threw Stockar a draft party, but Octavia was throwing up all day from the excitement. Or so she thought. A few days later, Octavia learned she was pregnant with the couple's second child.

McDougle signed a five-year, $7 million contract that summer and was ecstatic. After all the sacrifice, he would finally be able to take care of his family. It was four years before he'd saved up enough money to buy his wife a simple wedding band. And now, he could finally tell Octavia that her long hours working at the salon were over. He wanted her to quit and move with him to Detroit.

It was probably a blissfully proud moment for him. But Octavia had a business that was thriving. And anyone who has met her knows that Octavia is outgoing—a real people person. She wasn't the type to sit around a mansion admiring her jewelry or watching the help wax the Mercedes. But Stockar's offer was more ultimatum than request, so she decided to quit her business and give the housewife thing a try.

It didn't work.

"I had to give up everything I had worked for," she said. "My whole identity."

It wasn't just that she was used to being around people and she was suddenly isolated. Or that she missed the interaction with customers or the sense of satisfaction that came with doing a good job and seeing the appreciation in her customers' eyes. It was deeper than that.

"At that point, my whole life revolved around Stockar and his new job," she said. "I had nothing to do, so I started looking to him to fill a void in my life. I'd get up in the morning and say, 'OK, what am I going to cook for dinner today? What does he like to eat?' And I'd clean the house, and all I was trying to do was try to keep him happy because I had nothing else to do.

"So my expectations for him were, 'OK, I've been home all day. When you get off work, come straight home and let's do something together. Let's watch a movie. Whatever. Just get home after work.' Well, for him, he's excited he's playing pro football. He's got new teammates. So after work, he wants to hang out with his friends or maybe he wants to stop at the mall or maybe he'd come home and drop off his stuff and say, 'Hey, I'm going out with the O-line tonight.' And I'm like, 'What? What about me?' So it came to where we'd have petty arguments over stupid stuff like I would call his mom, who is a culinary art teacher, for his favorite recipes, and he'd come home and say, 'It doesn't taste right.' And I'd be devastated, and it would lead to an argument like, 'You ungrateful . . .' And the next day, I wouldn't want to cook anymore, and he'd come home and be like, 'Didn't you cook?' Arghhh!"

Octavia was talking to a close friend one day who told her point blank: "Octavia, you need a life."

Octavia agreed. She had made an honest effort to be a housewife. But it wasn't enough for her. "I learned early on that I can't just wait on him to make me happy," Octavia says.

For McDougle's first five NFL seasons, the family lived in Florida for six months and then moved to Detroit for six months. Octavia took her friend's advice and began taking real estate classes online and eventually got her license. She opened her own real estate office in 2001. Some of her first clients were the people she knew best—other NFL families. And this gave her invaluable insight and proved a great benefit to her family.

When players enter the league, she says, they buy five-bedroom, four-bath, four-car-garage homes that cost millions of dollars and have big mortgages. Octavia was getting their business on the back end of their NFL careers, usually a year or two after they were forced to hang up their cleats and they couldn't afford the payments any longer.

"They buy these big fancy homes, and then after the game, when all the fame is gone, there is a lot of strain on the family and on the marital relationship," she says. "After seeing the struggles older NFL couples were going through . . . I was like, 'Wow, I don't want to be like that.'"

It gave her an idea.

McDougle decided to specialize by working with athletes and their families and formed the Certified Sports and Entertainment Specialist designation to train Realtors so they understood the lifestyle transitions professional athletes go through.

"These guys are young, they don't have any formal financial background, and they have people giving them business ideas, investment opportunities. It's all so fast," Octavia says. "When their career comes to an end, what's going to replace the income or that lifestyle you had before? So you got a first-round guy, he's famous, everyone knows and loves him, and now it's over. What's he going to do with himself? What's he going to do to get that same respect from the community? When you are done, how are you going to pay your bills?"

Octavia was born in London and moved to America when she was nine. Her father passed away of an unknown heart ailment, and her mother thought it best that Octavia move to America to live with her grandmother, Gloria, until she could bring the rest of the family over. Gloria was very faithful, and that's where Octavia was first introduced to Christianity. Before long, she was a regular Sunday worshiper and member of the church choir.

She admits it was her faith in God and her desire to live a Christlike life that helped get her through the difficult times when she was apart from Stockar and later in her marriage when the challenges of living with an NFL player surfaced. Though they went through periods when they stopped going to church, or only attended sparingly, they never disconnected. Later, they decided to get more serious about their faith and saw it as an opportunity to take a spiritual journey together.

"You are always going to have trials and tribulations, no matter how much you try and follow the Word of God," Octavia shares.

They both relied on their faith to get them through some difficult times. They told God about their troubles, asked for His guidance, and worked at it.

"I had a lot going on," Octavia says. "I had my business, my kids, and now my husband comes home and he's demanding everything from me. There were times when our relationship was strained because he was used to being catered to hand and foot. He's a professional football player, but I don't look at him like that. I look at him as, 'Hey, you're my high school sweetheart. You're my best friend.'"

Octavia isn't just telling *her* story. She's telling the story of countless women all around the NFL. And perhaps corporate America too. Give a person enough power, celebrity, and adulation, and he or she is going to expect some of that at home as well.

Danisha Rolle, wife of former Tennessee Titans and Baltimore Ravens Pro Bowl defensive back Samari Rolle, worked in parenting intervention at Catholic Charities in Nashville and later earned a master's degree in clinical science and child therapy at Pepperdine University in Malibu, California. She wasn't a kept woman who needed a meal ticket. She was a self-starter and today is a successful publisher of *SET* magazine, a glossy quarterly publication that targets female sports fans and can be seen lying around athletes' lockers.

Though everyone likes a pat on the back, she says, some professional athletes have been getting a kiss on the behind as far back as elementary school.

It starts good-naturedly with proud parents showing support for their child. Then it expands to relatives who drive across town for a game and brag about their sweet little Walter Payton. High school coaches who want to build their own name on the backs of their teenage phenomenon follow. By ninth grade, the girls have discovered their sexual powers and start strutting their stuff for the school stud, and classmates learn that having an athlete drop by the house can make the lamest party really cool. "Stop by, whenever you want," they say. College recruiters follow, and the schools provide dates that masquerade as "campus escorts" for the boys. There is the rush of 70,000 to 100,000 fans screaming out his name after a big catch or a punishing tackle. More women . . . It's all free, right? More party invites. He gets tutors to help with his homework. NFL agents knock on his door, promising they'll get him the millions he deserves and the life he's always dreamed of.

It takes a strong person to remain grounded. It has nothing to do with education, race, or culture. Who among us wouldn't begin to feel entitled? It's not that the rest of us are better, more godly people. Most of us are just uglier and less talented.

This is where you can hear the echoes of coaches like Tony Dungy, Marvin Lewis, and Brad Childress talking about the importance of having men of faith on their rosters. These players understand there is something bigger than themselves and realize that someday they'll have to answer for their actions. The result is oftentimes a greater sense of humility, a willingness to think about the team over themselves, and the realization that their talent isn't their due, but rather a gift from God to be used for His purpose.

"As a football player, you have so many people feeding your ego and so many yes-men and cosigners that don't want to be cut off from the payroll," Danisha says. "That's where some of the stronger wives come in and say: 'Honey, now that you have a family, you can't pay for all of your friends' drinks and dinner anymore.' And because the wife is now the bad person who is pulling their banker away and cutting off the free rides, you get enemies real quick. It creates tension and disagreements because they are his friends and family and you are the bad woman he got hooked up with."

Cabrina Womack admits to having experienced the same pain and resentment. Former high school coaches were calling and asking Floyd for money. And she has a strained relationship with her own mother, partly because she wasn't willing to meet her mom's financial needs.

"The money is nice, but it puts an obligation on you," she says. "Because you have the money, you are supposed to help people out of their binds. A lot of players don't have relationships with their family members because of money.

"There was a time when Floyd's sister would vent at me. He was paying all her bills, and she was twenty-eight. And I told Floyd, 'Hey, it's time for her to be an adult.' So it breaks up relationships."

Corwin Anthony, Athletes in Action's pro ministry director, has heard these stories before. He says that of all the people who want something from an athlete—autographs, pictures, a jersey, a financial investment—none are as devious as family and friends.

"Almost every week in our couples Bible study we had to stop and counsel another couple who were expressing the pain and suffering that come from Momma wanting a new car, an uncle asking for money again, brothers trying to move into their house," Anthony says. "I remember talking to a rookie at camp once, and he got a phone call. He looked at the phone and recognized that the area code was from his hometown, and his head just dropped. Then he gathered himself, shook his head, and put the phone down. 'It's just somebody from my hometown wanting something again,' he said.

He's trying to make the team, and he's burdened when he sees a call from home. That's not right."

Anthony knows it is hard, but a player has to learn that no matter how much he loves them, his mother and father's job ended when he left home. He should honor his parents, Anthony acknowledges, but he is not obligated to support them for the rest of their lives.

These stories are legendary among the players. And the more money the player makes, the more the family expects him to pay its bills. It's like the family just hit the lotto.

"We had one mom who told her son, 'If your wife doesn't have to work, neither should we,' meaning herself and her other children. So this one guy was supporting five households because he felt obligated," Anthony says. "The players must understand the difference between helping and enabling. You are not helping them when you are enabling them to make poor choices with their money by replenishing the funds. And people wonder why these athletes end up bankrupt in retirement."

The demands of playing pro football, dealing with family and friends, the money, and the celebrity can really weigh on a player and his wife. If the couple doesn't work at the relationship and see it as a gift from God with its own set of trials, it can fall apart quite easily.

Octavia said that she would argue with Stockar even on the way to church sometimes, but that worship always helped them find a way to make up and keep their relationship strong.

Non-football couples find this to be true too.

"You might go in there with aggravation and frustration, and you're fussing at each other on the way there, but you go to the altar and you put your needs and wants before God and you say, 'Hey, Lord. Help me be a better spouse, more understanding, a better mom. Forgive me for being so difficult to deal with sometimes.' If you are really faithful, you can't walk out of there with those same issues in your heart," she says. "I also learned from going to church that when you say, 'OK, honey, I forgive you,' you have to truly forgive. You can't be like, 'Yeah, I forgive you,' but keep bringing it up every five minutes. Stockar and I are committed to one another and to going through this journey together."

Stockar's career lasted seven seasons and ended in Jacksonville when he ruptured his left Achilles tendon during practice in August 2007. Ironically it happened the same day his younger brother, Jerome, a first-round draft pick out of the University of Miami, ended his career with the New York Giants after tearing his triceps muscle during a preseason game against the Baltimore Ravens.

Since Stockar's retirement, the McDougles have undergone a complete role reversal, with Stockar at home supporting Octavia's career. The family has the real estate business and recently opened a vocational school called Beauty Anatomy as a community service initiative. According to Octavia, "It's a health, wellness, and cosmetology school and ties back to my early days when I was a hair dresser."

Stockar seemed to be adjusting to his life of leisure pretty well until one day he looked at his wife and said, "You know what? I'm bored. I need to get a job."

Octavia hesitated for a moment and said, "Why don't you be my assistant?"

Stockar thought about it. "Are you going to pay me?"

Octavia laughed at the irony. "Yeah, I'll pay you a salary."

Stockar paused to weigh the benefits—working from home, making his own hours, getting to kiss the boss.

"OK, then," he said.

GAME DAY

Game day is a big event for the entire family. Wives, children, grandparents, aunts and uncles, nieces and nephews make preparations to watch their homegrown star play on Sundays.

For the wives, though, it's often a juggling act.

Samari Rolle ended his eleven-year career with 385 solo tackles, 31 interceptions, and 9.5 quarterback sacks. For Rolle's family, Samari's performance had been a subject of discussion and excitement for more than two decades, beginning with his high school years at Miami Beach High School, then to college at Florida State University, and finally to the pros where he was selected by the then Tennessee Oilers in the second round of the 1998 draft.

The Saturday before the home games, the Rolles usually had family and friends over to their house. Samari would be there until he had to leave for the team hotel, and then Danisha was on her own. She'd have everyone up and fed by 11:00 a.m. Sunday, and they'd be out the door by 12:15 p.m. for the 1:00 p.m. start.

"Samari would call me before he went into the locker room or on the team bus, and we'd pray over the phone together before the game," Danisha says. "We would pray that God would protect all the players from both teams, and that He would allow Samari to have a great game. And we'd thank Him for Samari's gifts and talents, and we'd ask the Lord to use him however He saw fit."

The Rolles could afford a luxury suite and a driver by the time he signed a free agent contract with the Baltimore Ravens in 2005. After the game, the driver would take the family home while Danisha waited for her husband.

"We'd drive home together and discuss the game and how he played. That would be our time to recap, and he'd get calls from friends."

REALITY CHECK

When the players and their wives are outside the spotlight, they are usually the first to tell you that while celebrity has its moments, it's not the Cinderella tale it's made out to be.

Samari and Danisha were married in November 2003 in a

beautiful ceremony at the Vine Street Christian Church in Nashville. Samari had one child from a previous relationship, and the following year, Samari and Danisha had their first child together, a little boy named Jamir. It was a blessed event, as all births are, and the Rolles were delighted with their growing family. Twelve weeks later, Daddy was fired.

Ka-Blam! Just like that.

"I'm dealing with just having a baby," Danisha says. "I'd gained almost eighty pounds and had body image issues. We had one set of parents that were close to divorce. He's dealing with all these pressures to find a new team. And we couldn't communicate. Let me tell you, it doesn't matter how much money you have or how big a star your husband is, that's a tough time."

The couple had arguments. One turned into a fight where Samari's watchband broke and cut Danisha's eye, sending her to the emergency room. The hospital contacted police, and Rolle was arrested on a charge of simple assault, a misdemeanor.

"We had to learn from that experience," Danisha admits. "It was during that period that we really had to rely on our faith in God; that He would provide for us and get us through our troubles. What we learned is that you can't close one another off. Many men will close off instead of talking; they won't tell their spouse what they are thinking and feeling. [Women] withdraw and essentially do the same thing.

"We spoke with many couples, friends and . . . you come into marriage with this idea of 'happily ever after' where you love one another and never argue, and then once you're married you realize that's not the case.

"When we were dating, I'd hear other men say, 'Oh, I love her, but I hate her sometimes too.' And I would think to myself, *I don't believe this guy could really love his wife if he thinks that way.* But that's not reality. When you are dating, it's easy to say, 'I'm outta here,' and leave. But when you're married, you can't just walk out on your husband and children and the life you've made and quit. It takes the strongest couples to say, 'Listen, you can't respond to me this way when you are angry.' And when you have children, you can't throw things and get upset and walk out. This is part of growing up and maturing, and it hits us at a time when we are earning a lot of money and in the public spotlight. So mistakes get noticed."

Danisha, one of eleven children, was introduced to her faith through her parents, who were very active in their church in Evanston, Illinois. She met Samari at Florida State, where she earned a degree in psychology. Family has always been a big part of Danisha's life. Samari and Danisha now have four children, two boys and two girls ages five to eleven.

In Samari's final years in Baltimore, they would attend Bible study in a small room at the Ravens training facility, where they would talk about the accountability they had in their walk with Christ and about being a champion of the faith.

Danisha liked couples Bible study because they could bounce ideas off one another, because they could apply the lessons of the Bible to what they were facing in their daily lives, and because it provided reinforcement at a time when the distractions and temptations of life could be overwhelming. Without friends or co-workers to share experiences with, Danisha admits that it can be easy to get off track and return to ungodly ways.

"You go through life and you pick up little things that will strengthen your faith, but to go to Bible study and hear it and see people nodding in agreement and to see that they have the same questions you do, it feels good to be in that environment and have the understanding of other people."

THE GLUE

Dionne Boldin met her husband, Anquan, in high school when they went to rival schools, and the relationship continued at Florida State University where they dated on and off. "He had a name in sports, but he was just a quiet, humble person, and that intrigued me," she says. As is the case with many people, both of their relationships with God were up and down during college as they fought to battle the pressures of young adulthood and still tried to maintain their faith.

She led the Ravens' wives study in 2010 and assigned the book *Having a Mary Heart in a Martha World* by Joanna Weaver, about balancing one's hectic life while spending time with God. The takeaway was that you have to make time to worship.

Boldin says a number of women confided that they suffered from depression and identity crisis. After giving up their own careers to follow their husbands, they lost their self-confidence and sense of purpose. One woman had gone to law school, but she never took the bar exam. She'd expected to be a practicing lawyer with kids. Instead, she was hopping around from team to team with her husband.

When Boldin hears other wives talk about giving up promising careers to follow their husbands, she understands. She has a bachelor's and master's in psychology and was ready to begin working in the school system. But she never did. "I was passionate about it. I loved it. But it never worked out," she shares.

"That was something I struggled with. Who was I supposed to be? There was a point where I felt like it wasn't enough to be his wife and the mother of two kids. I had these dreams, and they kind of disappeared."

Another issue that affected the wives in her Ravens group was depression caused by the husband's infidelity and the resulting "What's wrong with me?" issues. There were also women in the group who were engaged to players they couldn't get to the altar. Child rearing was always a topic of consternation. And sometimes, finances and the team's pecking order were discussed. That's something Rolle had experienced too.

"There is a point where you want to keep up with the Joneses," she admits. "There is a certain pressure to look like a status symbol, whether that means buying the latest limited-edition bag or not living in a townhouse. Some of that pressure can be alleviated by the teams. Some clubs encourage the guys to hang out together and they supply the teams with a list of telephone numbers and addresses so you can get together and you invite teammates for birthday parties. Other organizations operate very differently. You have a millionaires' row in the locker room. That extends to the way families are perceived."

Boldin knows she lives a good life with many of the perks other women—and men for that matter—wish they had. But she could do without the scrutiny and criticism. Sometimes she wonders what life would be like if she could swap all the fame and fortune for a little normalcy.

"There is a part of the public that feels you are living the dream. And others think, *Oh, you are just hanging on to his coattails.* I get a little of both. It would surprise a lot of people how much the wives depend on our faith to work through our problems while being so much in the spotlight," she says. "I think that 99 percent of us, if we could just have a normal life where nobody cared about us, we'd be happy with that.

"By growing with Christ, I have come to realize that if my role at this point is to be a mother and to raise two boys, so be it. My husband is not around a lot. Down the line, I aspire to other things. Right now, I'm comfortable with being the glue."

THE FAMILY PSYCHOLOGIST

Jasmin Stuckey was living in Philadelphia when a friend introduced her to Chansi Stuckey, a New York Jets wide receiver two years her junior. He opened doors, had a good sense of humor, asked her opinion. He didn't carry himself with the "I'm the big man" cockiness that some young athletes have, and that was attractive to Jasmin. She had seen a lot in life and wasn't a pushover for a jock. She had earned a finance degree from St. John's University in Queens, New York, was the mother of a small child from a previous relationship, owned a home, and had held jobs in real estate, finance, and fashion writing.

After their marriage in October 2010, life became a whirlwind of change.

Chansi was selected by the New York Jets in the seventh round of the 2007 draft out of Clemson University. He spent the season on injured reserve with a foot injury, but bounced back in 2008 with 32 receptions for 359 yards and 3 touchdowns. In 2009, he was traded to the Cleveland Browns four games into the season. And the following year showed promise, finishing third on the team with 40 receptions for 346 yards.

It was a good time for Stuckey to be entering free agency. In the summer of 2011, he signed a two-year, $3.5 million free agent contract with the Cardinals that included a $700,000 signing bonus.

The young couple had been looking to buy a place in Arizona and were talking about having a baby the morning she met the other Cardinals wives at Lynette's house for their Thursday Bible study.

Now, two years into the NFL lifestyle, Jasmin says one of her most important tasks is supporting her husband and helping him keep the right emotional state of mind. Stuckey had a nagging hamstring injury early in the 2011 season and finished the year with just 4 receptions for 39 yards and no touchdowns.

The contract is a lot of money by regular-people standards, but it's not a huge commitment for an NFL team. A club that invests big money in a player is going to give him every opportunity to succeed. It's not just the money. Some executive put his name and reputation behind the draft pick or big-money signing, and he doesn't just *want* the player to succeed—he *needs* him to succeed for the benefit of his *own* career. Those guys get second and third chances.

That's not the case with Stuckey, who has bounced from one team to the next, never quite convincing his coaches to make a long-term financial commitment. Every day, every practice, every catch is a reminder of what he's capable of, and every drop puts him that much closer to the waiver wire. It can drive you a little nuts.

"I have to be his psychologist, emotionally ready and stable to deal with whatever he's coming home with," says Jasmin. "I was surprised by how much emotional support they require. It's not only him; it's the million-dollar guys and their wives too."

She thought it would be different in Arizona. The Cardinals had shown interest and paid Chansi a nice signing bonus. She'd finally be able to take a deep breath and relax. Or so she thought. The offer meant they were interested. It didn't mean they were entering a committed relationship. This is the NFL, as in Not For Long. They could cut Stuckey the day after he signed his contract and the only thing the team would lose is the signing bonus. The "sweet ride" she imagined when Chansi signed the agreement, according to Jasmin, changed once he got to camp.

"Even though he signed a two-year deal with a bonus, we still felt like we were trying to compete and make the team even after all of that. And it wears down on your self-esteem and self-confidence," she shares. "So when he is coming home and he is unsure, immediately that makes me anxious and that makes me get scared to death, but I can't be that way. I have to be the strong one. And that's when a lot of the prayer comes in. We pray every night together."

Jasmin said the couple asks God for clarity in their lives so they can make the right choices, and they reassure Him that they will maintain their faith no matter what His plan is for their family.

"There is no job security from one day to the next," Jasmin says. "If you have a regular job, unless you throw the stapler at your boss's head, chances are that you are still going to have a job come Monday."

The NFL is a tough place. And while the insecurity provides tremendous motivation, it also changes people. The way a coach says good morning is rerun in a player's mind over and over.

Did he seem happy to see me? . . . Was it a disappointed hello, like he had to say hi because we were the only people in the hall? I think he avoided eye contact. Crap. I'm going to get cut.

Sometimes an unenthusiastic coach is just constipated. Or maybe he caught his daughter making out with her boyfriend on the sofa. Or he didn't sleep well, or . . . who knows? This isn't something that's exclusive to the NFL. It happens in factory lunch rooms, corporate gyms, and everywhere else that workers and managers interact all over America. The difference is that most of us have a little more job security, whereas the NFL is a day-to-day commitment. When they call you an at-will employee, they aren't kidding.

"Chansi has a tendency to overanalyze," Jasmin admits. "He gets worried about how the guys upstairs are perceiving him. He wants to make sure he is putting his best foot forward, and that they know he is giving 100 percent every day. He'll start picking stuff apart, and I'll say we can't really worry about it; we have to pray about it.

"Let me tell you, there have been days where he fumbled the ball, and I have cried in front of the television. But I got all my cry out and had a smile on my face when he came home. I can't show him that I'm afraid," she says.

"He's a new husband, but he's also a new father. So he's a new leader for the household. That's also something he deals with—being the man and taking care of everything, so I don't want to make him feel inadequate if I'm scared. I don't want him to feel like he's not enough for us. So I pray on these things and support him as much as I know how."

ASKING FOR HELP

The Cardinals' wives-only Bible study is winding down. And Jasmin is telling the story of how she spent much of her early childhood living at her grandmother's home in Camphill, Alabama, about twenty minutes from Auburn University, where she attended church most Sundays.

When she returned to live with her mother in Philadelphia during her high school years, Jasmin strayed from her religious foundation.

"Throughout my life, I've always heard God telling me one thing, and then I just do what I want to do. I do what makes me happy. So what I got out of our Bible study was the idea of obedience. When you are a child, you are obedient to your parents. Right now, it means coming to God with a childlike attitude and submitting to Him."

The wake-up call that sent Jasmin back to Christ eight years ago was the birth of her daughter, Kiersten, in April 2004. It forced Jasmin to look at the decisions she'd made in her life. She went to her grandmother for advice and was told that when we are not listening to God and we are living by our own wants and desires, He will put us in a situation that sends us running back to Him.

When Jasmin was pregnant, she was all alone. Who else could she go to other than God? she shares with the wives.

"When I was in college, I had this belief that you needed to get your life together before you could go back to church. I thought I needed to work on myself. I had it totally screwed up. You go to church so you *can* get your life together. When I had my daughter, that's when I really focused on getting back to God. And I've been going to church regularly."

BETTER MOTHERS, FRIENDS, SIBLINGS

Dreama Graves concludes the Bible study by asking the women to start a journal so they can write down their thoughts on the book and the lessons they are learning about hearing God. In addition to the readings, she asks the ladies to read Proverbs 31:10–31, where the Bible describes the qualities of a wife with noble character:

> *A wife of noble character who can find?*
> *She is worth far more than rubies.*
> *Her husband has full confidence in her*
> *and lacks nothing of value.*
> *She brings him good, not harm,*
> *all the days of her life.*
> *She selects wool and flax*
> *and works with eager hands.*
> *She is like the merchant ships,*
> *bringing her food from afar.*
> *She gets up while it is still night;*
> *she provides food for her family*
> *and portions for her female servants.*
> *She considers a field and buys it;*
> *out of her earnings she plants a vineyard.*
> *She sets about her work vigorously;*
> *her arms are strong for her tasks.*
> *She sees that her trading is profitable,*
> *and her lamp does not go out at night.*
> *In her hand she holds the distaff*
> *and grasps the spindle with her fingers.*
> *She opens her arms to the poor*
> *and extends her hands to the needy.*
> *When it snows, she has no fear for her household;*
> *for all of them are clothed in scarlet.*
> *She makes coverings for her bed;*
> *she is clothed in fine linen and purple.*
> *Her husband is respected at the city gate,*
> *where he takes his seat among the elders of the land.*

She makes linen garments and sells them,
  and supplies the merchants with sashes.
She is clothed with strength and dignity;
  she can laugh at the days to come.
She speaks with wisdom,
  and faithful instruction is on her tongue.
She watches over the affairs of her household
  and does not eat the bread of idleness.
Her children arise and call her blessed;
  her husband also, and he praises her:
"Many women do noble things,
  but you surpass them all."
Charm is deceptive, and beauty is fleeting;
  but a woman who fears the LORD *is to be praised.*
Honor her for all that her hands have done,
  and let her works bring her praise at the city gate.

Every week they read part of the book and discuss a few chapters. "The goal by the end of the season," Graves says, "is that we will be hearing from God in a bigger, clearer way, feeling confident that we are hearing Him and obeying what we are hearing."

Each year, the Graves family performs community outreach. One year they supported families with loved ones in Iraq by inviting them to a Cardinals game. Another year, they contacted shelters that specialize in helping battered women. The Bible study group adopted Dreama's cause in 2011 and dedicated some of their weekly Bible studies to working with women at the shelter.

"We want to hear from God, and we want to be better wives, better mothers, better siblings, better friends. We want to be more complete women by the end of the season," Dreama says.

4

OVERCOMING ADVERSITY

Blessed is the one who perseveres under trial because, having stood the test, that person will receive the crown of life that the Lord has promised to those who love him.

—James 1:12

NFL players appear to be living the perfect life: money, celebrity, and a public that worships them. As we've seen in earlier chapters, the reality is much different from the images we see on television and in glossy magazines. All the money and fame doesn't protect them from the same painful life experiences that ordinary folks endure every day. No one knows that better than New York Jets running back LaDainian Tomlinson or former Baltimore Ravens quarterback Trent Dilfer. Both were voted to the Pro Bowl. Dilfer won a Super Bowl title with the Ravens. And Tomlinson is a lock to be enshrined in the Pro Football Hall of Fame once his career ends.

What these world-class athletes have in common is that each was brought to his knees by sickness and death, and in their worst moments, neither turned to the NFL commissioner or their adoring fans for salvation. In their very darkest hours—alone, weeping, and scared—they each in turn looked to the heavens and begged for God's mercy and understanding.

While neither of these men fully understands why they had to suffer, perhaps it was in part so that the rest of us could learn from the experience.

UNDERSTANDING GOD'S PAIN

Trent Dilfer had taken his family to Disneyland for a short vacation with Mickey and Minnie in the spring of 2003 when his five-year-old son, Trevin, caught a virus and became feverish. After a doctor diagnosed him with asthma and bronchitis, Dilfer, who quarterbacked the Baltimore Ravens to a 34–7 victory over the New York Giants in the 2001 Super Bowl, packed up his family and returned home.

Trevin was fine on the trip back, but the next day he was struggling to speak. While Trent was out with his daughters—Madeleine, Victoria, and Delaney—his wife, Cass, took Trevin to the emergency room.

The doctors said it could be hepatitis and sent him to a local children's hospital for observation. On the way there, his heart stopped in the ambulance. The medical crew revived him, but it stopped again at the hospital. When Dilfer arrived at his son's room, the little boy was surrounded by male nurses, his chest was cut open, and a doctor was manually pumping his little heart.

Doctors told Trent and Cass that Trevin had caught a rare virus; their son's heart was failing, and there wasn't anything medically they could do about it. That's when the seriousness of what was happening hit them like a thunderbolt.

"You don't really know how to handle it," Dilfer says. "Everything is a blur. It happens, and you follow what the doctors tell you. You pray. They are telling you that your son is really sick and he might die. But we were just at Disneyland. The kids were happy. You look around trying to sort it all out. There was a lawn chair in the emergency room. I don't know why. The doctors are telling us there is nothing they can do. He's not going to make it? What?"

The doctors put Trevin on a heart-lung bypass machine to keep him alive. It was a short-term fix. They needed to get him to the hospital at Stanford University in Palo Alto, California, but the medical equipment was sensitive and the tubes and wires connected to Trevin's chest could slip off at any time. They needed a medical helicopter to fly him to the hospital, but the US was in the middle of the Iraq War and all the helicopters were overseas with the troops.

The doctors decided they were out of options; they'd have to put Trevin in an ambulance and drive him to Stanford. The doctors warned Trent and Cass that they had never used the unit in an ambulance before and it wasn't a great idea. It was a miracle their son had gotten this far, and it would probably take another one for him to get to the hospital alive. Any bump in the road, a hard stop, anything, and the unit could detach and Trevin would die in the ambulance.

The Dilfers followed behind in a separate car driven by Trent's friend Brad Bell. For three and a half hours, they drove with lights flashing, sirens blaring. The whole way, they watched the back of the ambulance for bodies to suddenly begin moving frantically inside.

"It was a numb, surreal feeling," Dilfer says. "We prayed the whole time."

When they pulled up in front of the hospital, there was a tremendous sense of relief. They had made it and were hoping the new doctors could figure something out. Instead, they told Dilfer that the machine was so fragile, they weren't sure Trevin would survive until they got him to his room a few flights up in an elevator. Even then, they'd have to put a new machine on him. Each step was life-threatening, they warned.

"It was a series of five nail-biting moments that he had to survive, and we made it through each one of them," Dilfer shares. "It had been like this for twelve or fourteen consecutive hours. I remember just falling to my knees and saying, 'Lord, I can't hold on to this. You already got him farther than we thought You'd get him. He is completely in Your hands; there is nothing we can do. Prepare me for whatever is coming.'"

REBELLION

Dilfer came from a broken home in Santa Cruz, California. Though he went to church and accepted Christ at ten, there was a lot of residual pain from his parents' breakup. By his junior year in high school, Dilfer, an A student who starred in football, baseball, and basketball, began to rebel. He was so successful that his drinking and partying went largely unnoticed or were overlooked by coaches, teachers, and family members; everyone was so thrilled when he was offered a scholarship to play football at Fresno State.

College doesn't usually have the effect of lessoning a kid's desire to party or his access to drugs, alcohol, or women. They are aplenty and, to well-known athletes, usually free.

Dilfer's partying increased when he tore a muscle in his arm his freshman year and was redshirted—meaning he couldn't play, but that the year didn't count against his four years of eligibility. He was under the radar and making all the wrong sorts of friends.

The following season, Dilfer was healthy again and earned the starting job at Fresno State. He really lived the life of the big man on campus. The team's winning record coupled with his good grades covered up the fact that he was out of control. He was drinking, womanizing, getting in fights; he wasn't in a good place.

"At that time in my life, it was all about me, me, me," Dilfer admits. "But I still had that craving for something better and an emptiness in my soul."

Trent would feel occasional guilt over his behavior and would drop by the Evangelical Free Church on campus from time to time. That's where he met Joe Broussard, the Fresno State athletic department's team chaplain and the college director of the Evangelical Free Church.

The summer after Trent's redshirt freshman year, Broussard, who would later preside over Trent and Cass's wedding, stopped by Trent's apartment to ask if he would work as a counselor at a camp run by the Fellowship of Christian Athletes.

"He took a risk, because while I was expressing my faith, I was still unsure about it. He knew what was going on in my life. He took the risk of having me go down there as a counselor when I should have probably been a camper," Dilfer says.

The counselors met about two days before the campers arrived, and Trent found himself hanging out with other students who were "living authentic lives for God, and I was so turned on by it, just the wholeness they had in their lives. It's what I was missing."

That's when Dilfer says he made the decision to get serious about his faith. When he returned from camp, he felt changed and wanted to be around like-minded individuals. One who came to mind was a pretty classmate named Cassandra Franzman, the captain of the swim team. He'd first noticed her when they had a class together and the professor was attacking Christianity pretty hard. Cassandra took on the professor, standing up for her faith. It got Trent's attention. They'd dated once, but she thought he was a goofball and he could only muster a friendship after that. She knew what Trent was up to off the field and had wisely kept him at arm's length. So after attending the camp, Trent went to her and said he was trying to clean up his life and didn't want to hang out with the same people anymore. He needed a friend.

She didn't buy it at first. But in a short time, she saw that he was genuinely trying to change his life. This version of Dilfer was a pretty good guy. The two started hanging out, sharing their ideas about life and faith, and she eventually broke up with her boyfriend to be with Trent. Six months later they were engaged, and five months after that they were married. He was twenty-one.

Dilfer declared for the NFL draft after his redshirt junior season and was selected by the Tampa Bay Buccaneers with the sixth overall pick in 1994. He held out in a contract dispute and played poorly his rookie season, starting just two games and passing for one touchdown and six interceptions.

He got better and in 1997 became the first Bucs quarterback to be voted to the Pro Bowl after passing for 2,555 yards, throwing 21 TDs, and leading the team to its first play-off game in fifteen seasons. Dilfer broke his collarbone in November 1999, and backup Shaun King led the team to four wins in its final five games and took the team to the NFC championship where it lost 11–6 to St. Louis. After the season, the team declined to pick up Dilfer's option.

He signed a free agent contract with the Baltimore Ravens, which turned out to be one of the best moves of his career.

The Ravens had the league's best defense, holding opponents to an NFL-record 165 points behind stars like linebacker Ray Lewis, defensive end Michael McCrary, and safety Rod Woodson. When Baltimore won the Super Bowl that season, Dilfer—who completed 12 of 25 passes for 153 yards and one touchdown in the championship—didn't get any credit for the win. The defense tied a Super Bowl record with four interceptions, and Ray Lewis was named the game's Most Valuable Player. Two months after the season ended, the Ravens decided against keeping Dilfer as their quarterback and signed free agent Elvis Grbac to a five-year contract. It was embarrassing and shocking and still pains Dilfer to this day.

He signed a free agent contract with the Seattle Seahawks in 2001 and went 4-0 after starter Matt Hasselbeck was injured. Coach Mike Holmgren was so impressed that he named Dilfer the starter the following season and signed him to a four-year contract.

The Seahawks were on the rise and this was supposed to be Dilfer's big break, but he sprained his knee in the preseason opener and was lost for the year after tearing his right Achilles tendon in Week 7. That's all it would take for Hasselbeck to reclaim the starting job. Dilfer would later ask for a trade and join the Cleveland Browns in 2005. That same season, Hasselbeck guided the Seahawks to their first Super Bowl in franchise history.

A SENSE OF PEACE

Trevin was Dilfer's only son, the only other man in a house full of women. He loved to hang out with his daddy in the locker room and often challenged Trent's teammates to footraces. He had blond hair and was all of about fifty pounds when the virus felled him. The surprise, doctors later told Dilfer, was that it went to his heart. That's not common.

Trevin was in pain and was kept sedated while in the hospital. Doctors said he needed a heart transplant, but to get on the list he had to prove he had brain activity. They reduced the sedative so he could feel.

"I knew he could hear us. His eyes would flicker. He could grip a little bit, like the slightest touch in his fingertips, but he was in a ton of pain when he did it so we only allowed it to happen one time," Dilfer said.

They put him on the list for a heart donation.

For the next twenty-five days, friends and family would visit to support Trent and Cass and to pray over their little boy. Any sort of infection would reduce the chances of a successful transplant and would kick Trevin off the donor list. Every day that passed had its worries, and of course, though no one wanted to think about it, everyone was waiting for some other family to suffer the most horrific event of their lives so Trevin could get a heart.

Trent and Cass would stand at the end of their little boy's bed and rub his feet. Trevin's sisters, who were staying with their grandparents, talked into a tape recorder so he could hear their voices and know that his sisters loved him and that they weren't far away.

Then, they sat and waited.

While Cass could patiently sit in the room for hours, Trent had a hard time with it and would go to the hospital's rooftop garden or to the chapel for prayer.

Dilfer had made millions of dollars. He'd been to the summit of the game he loved. Was God saying, "Wait a minute. Not so fast"? Dilfer says he never went there. He'd recommitted to Christ in college; he'd repented and never looked back.

When Trent and Cass returned from Easter services, there were doctors from the intensive care and cardiac units in Trevin's room. It was bad news. He had a systemic infection and probably had only a few more days to live.

On April 24, Trent told Cass he'd sit with Trevin so she could spend her birthday with the girls. For Trent, it was time to be alone with Trevin and to say his good-byes. He sat next to the bed and, through periods of heavy sobbing, composed a two-page letter to his baby boy.

Of all the memories Dilfer has of Trevin's sickness, this is the one that still makes him cry when he speaks of it. It was the most intense, emotional period he ever experienced.

"I woke up early that morning and spent a lot of time in solitude, pouring out my heart to God," he remembers. "I prayed with Trevin. I talked to him and told him how much he meant to me and how much I loved him."

Up to that point, Dilfer says, he had dealt with a lot of his own pain, but he had never confronted his wife's pain or his family's pain. They were all suffering, but he'd been doing everything he could to keep it together. He needed a clear head to make decisions about his son's medical care. He had to compartmentalize his feelings so he could be strong for his wife and daughters and allow them to experience their own pain. This required him to keep some emotional distance from the events surrounding him.

But on this day, it all came crashing down. And what Dilfer remembers the most, and the reason he believes he still gets so emotional, is that for the first time in his life he had an inkling of what God must have felt when He watched the life drain slowly from His Son suffering on that cross.

"It was in those moments that He revealed to me His pain for mankind," Dilfer says. "It is so much more painful to hurt for others than to hurt for yourself. That was the day that I allowed the pain of my wife and my girls and Trevin to hit me. God painted this incredible picture through this experience of His pain for us. Of His sacrifice for us. And it was so intense and so life changing. God allowed me the experience of not just knowing my own pain, but the pain of the ones I love the most."

In those final days, Steve Stenstrom, a former NFL quarterback who runs a campus ministry at Stanford, put Trent and Cass in touch with a man who had lost his daughter a year earlier. He gave the Dilfers a piece of advice that they have followed ever since.

"He told us, 'The same spirit that lives in you, Trent, and in you, Cass, is not divided. There is no conflict in the Holy Spirit. So when you are asking for peace on a decision, it's not the right decision until you both have the same peace.'

"It's so simple, but it's so enlightening," Dilfer says. "That was the day I developed a peace and decided it was the right thing for Trevin to turn off his life support." Doctors had said that Trevin could live another two weeks at most, but that he'd be in pain until the very end.

"[Cass] was like, 'No, no, no, we're going to keep fighting.' And I was wise enough to realize my decision was not the right decision because we were not unified. So we kept praying together for unity."

A day passed, and they were still holding vigil at Trevin's side, waiting and praying, when Cass went into a back room the hospital furnished with bunks and other items.

She had been gone for a bit when suddenly Trent heard terrible groans, followed by screams and shouts coming from inside the room. He grew concerned and ran to the door where he heard furniture being moved and objects thumping on the floor.

She was in the room by herself, but she wasn't alone. The heavenly Father she'd loved and trusted all her life had come to wrench her son from her arms, and she wasn't about to let go without a screaming, clawing, knockdown fight.

"I was scared," Trent admits in a tired, emotionless voice. "I had never heard this from my wife. It was so painful to hear her wrestling with God."

The room quieted. Cass was drained.

"She came out with a peace of 'OK, it's good now.' And it was at that time, after she had dealt with God on a personal level, that it unified our hearts that this was the right thing to do."

The morning of April 27, Trent and Cass took the girls to the garden on the roof of the hospital and told them they were going to let Trevin go home to God.

The oldest, Maddie, screamed and told her parents they were ruining her life. Once things settled down, the family went back down to Trevin's room and played his favorite song for him. It's called "One of These Days" by FFH and is about dying and going to heaven.

There were four people in the room: Trent, Cass, Trevin, and a nurse. Trent turned off the machine. And Trevin passed away quietly. From the time he got feverish to the day he died, it was forty days.

"I never asked why," says Dilfer. "I've never been obsessed with what it was or why it happened."

Dilfer believes that God is loving and merciful and that there must have been something at play that he couldn't comprehend.

Who could comprehend good coming out of so much suffering?

Forty days of praying. Forty days of hoping God would save his son. Forty days of offering his own life in exchange for an innocent little boy who never had a chance to see all the joy and wonder life on earth offers. For nothing.

It begs the question: Why pray if in your greatest hour of need, God is not there for you? It's a fair question.

"The truth of God's Word is that this is not our home," Dilfer painfully acknowledges. "If the motivation for your faith is what's going on in the seventy-five or ninety years we have here on earth, then you are missing the truth of God's promises. What God promises is eternity. This is not our home. When we make the decision to trust in Him and to follow Him, our home is with Him for eternity."

Dilfer says that when Trevin died, he experienced a peace that is hard to describe. He understands the skeptics will have a field day with that statement, but he's OK with that. He doesn't get upset by those who question him because he understands that unless you live it, it's difficult to grasp. How can a man who just lost his beloved son feel peace?

"There is a Bible verse that's resonated with me from the time this happened and every day since in my struggles," Dilfer shares. "'And the peace of God, which transcends all understanding, will guard your hearts and your minds in Christ Jesus'[Philippians 4:7].

"I will stand on the rooftops and scream out that, yes, I lost my five-year-old son, my only son. I faced life's greatest tragedy. But without a shadow of a doubt, I have experienced that promise of a peace that transcends understanding. I can't always articulate it. I can't explain it. I can't fathom it at times.

"I can't fathom that as we turned life support off and I saw devastation in my wife and felt it myself, at the same exact moment we had this incredible peace of what was happening and we continued to have a peace and my daughters who live faithful lives have a peace. I don't know how else to say it. Is it a supernatural occurrence when the Holy Spirit of God lives in you and you choose to be obedient to Him? People say that makes no sense. That it's crazy. And I get it. I get their skepticism. I've experienced a supernatural occurrence in my life, and it's inexplicable."

THE LESSON

It's been nine years since Trevin's death. He'd be nearly fifteen now and probably following in his daddy's footsteps playing football in the Stanford area. Instead, Trent and Cass are following Maddie, who has become quite a volleyball player and is being scouted by Division 1 programs.

The family speaks of Trevin more easily now. Something will happen around the house, and Trent or Cass will say, "Remember the time Trevin . . ." without getting teary-eyed. The girls have come to terms with their brother's death, too, and are maturing into beautiful, smart young ladies who are living their own lives with their own hopes and dreams for the future.

Their recovery from Trevin's death took time, though. "When my kids get sick, it is horrific," Dilfer says. The family moved just outside Palo Alto a few years ago. "We live twenty minutes from where Trevin died. We've been back to the hospital twice. When [Delaney] was four or five, she had to have her gallbladder taken out. The room was directly above the room Trevin died in. We had to walk the halls for five days while she had the gallbladder taken out, and there were complications with the anesthesia. I mean, revisiting that, to go there for doctors' appointments with my kids at the same hospital. To see the nurses. We are confronted with this all the time. I still fight a lot of this stuff, but what God impresses on my heart is, *Why don't you get it? It's so much bigger than the present stuff you are dealing with.*"

When Trevin died, he was five and a half, and his youngest sister Delaney was one. He had been a little rough around the edges at first, but after she was born he "softened up like a cupcake," says his father. Overnight, she was the greatest thing that ever happened in his life. He'd become someone's big brother after all, and that's quite a responsibility.

What's weird, Trent says, is that Delaney is the spitting image of Trevin in every way.

"She looks like him, she's built like him, she acts like him, she talks like him, her eyes are this grayish-blue, which are like his," Trent reflects. "Every day we look at her, we see Trevin. It's crazy. I appreciate God's little nuisances and how He manifests Himself in a million different aspects of life."

Dilfer, who now works as a football analyst for ESPN, says he's had time to heal and gain perspective on Trevin's life and all the lives his son touched.

"The takeaway for me is that so many things that we put a tremendous value on while we are here on earth pale in comparison to the eternal value of our souls," Dilfer says. "Even—and this is the one people really freak out with—even our kids.

"You gotta let go because they are not ours. They are a gift, they are a responsibility, they are treasures, but we don't own them. Ultimately God holds us in His hands, and He has ownership.

"The more I learn to let go of the things that are important to me in life, the more clearly I begin to understand how much God loves me and loves us and values our eternal state so much more than our present state.

"And yet, He still allows us great experiences while we are here. We should live life to the fullest. We shouldn't live life indifferently. There is tremendous value in what we do with our time here. But it is all a backdrop to our eternal lives. I get it now. That is the wisdom that has come from all this."

And the God of all grace, who called you to his eternal glory in Christ, after you have suffered a little while, will himself restore you and make you strong, firm and steadfast. (1 Peter 5:10)

"I CAN'T FIND THE HEARTBEAT"

LaDainian and LaTorsha Tomlinson returned home after the 2005 Pro Bowl and went to the doctor for a checkup. LaTorsha was pregnant with the couple's first child, a little girl they would name Mckiah Renee, and like all young couples, the Tomlinsons were overwhelmed with pride and excitement as they made plans to start their new family. With each visit to the doctor's office, Mckiah would grow bigger, and they would marvel at the little miracle growing inside her mother's tummy. Her birth was scheduled for May, just a few months after her father had one of the best seasons of his career, scoring a league-high 17 rushing touchdowns, finishing fifth in the league with 1,776 total yards from scrimmage, and earning his second Pro Bowl invitation. For the powerful running back with a 1,000-watt smile, life couldn't have been any better. The good Lord seemed to give LaDainian two helpings of everything: good looks, athletic talent, money, a pretty wife, and now, a little girl to spoil into his old age.

That's how the world saw it anyway.

God had something else in mind. The doctor's visit that started ordinarily enough was about to change the Tomlinsons' lives forever. The date was February 22, 2005.

"I remember the doctor saying, 'Hmm, that's weird. I can't find the heartbeat,'" Tomlinson says. "He said, 'Let me go get another doctor. Maybe I just can't see it or something.' So another doctor comes in. And he says he can't find the heartbeat either. And then you start to sense that something really bad is happening."

The couple rushed to the hospital where doctors again tried to find a heartbeat. *God, please look out for our little girl*, Tomlinson thought. But the baby's fate had been sealed days or even weeks earlier.

"I never asked God why," Tomlinson says. "My first thought was to make sure my wife got through this. I felt like I had to be really strong in front of her. And I tried to make some sense of it and see some positive. I don't know how the thoughts came into my head. You just can't believe what's happening in that moment. I remember saying to her, 'Everything happens for a reason, even if we can't understand it now. God has a plan.'"

"She asked, 'Why does this have to happen?' . . . She said, 'This is not fair.'" One can only imagine how confused they were. A couple in their midtwenties, riding on top of the world, faithful in their belief in God and His plan for their lives. . . . Did they do something wrong? Were they being punished? L.T. had made many right decisions in his life, worked so hard to be successful. He had always wanted to be a family man, always dreamed of kids, chose his wife in part because he thought she'd make a great mother. What happened? The last time the world saw L.T., he was racking up the yards and flashing that high-wattage smile—but that's just entertainment. This was the real stuff. Just him, trying to console the woman he loved more than life itself, while fighting back his own grief and trying to stay strong for everyone else.

"I said [to LaTorsha], 'What if I was to tell you our baby girl was to be born, and a year later, we'd lose her then? . . . What if she had something wrong with her like a disease that would give us challenges for the rest of our lives?'" He was trying to ease his wife's pain by finding some good in a horrible, unexplainable event, the best he could. "That's kind of how I started to deal with the fact that it wasn't going to happen at that time," he said. "We weren't going to have a baby now. OK. But I always felt like it would happen for us, and we'd have children and a family.

"I cried when I was by myself. When I was driving, I shed tears. It was rough on me, too, but I leaned on what I always knew—my faith. That's the foundation in my life. My faith tells me that everything happens for a reason and that God doesn't make mistakes. It just wasn't going to happen *now*."

L.T. delayed his off-season workouts and spent time with his wife while she continued to grieve. Miscarriages occur in 15 to 20 percent of known pregnancies, according to the Mayo Clinic, but that's little consolation to the families suffering through the loss.

When Tomlinson's pain was at its worst, he found solace in the belief that God had a plan for his life and that's what allowed him to move forward. Instead of dwelling on his daughter's death, he decided to focus on the parts of his life that he could control.

As the 2005 season unfolded, LaDainian had a great purpose in his life. His goal was to be the best running back to ever play the game . . . and he and LaTorsha had privately decided to try and get pregnant again. Family meant everything to them, and LaDainian and LaTorsha were certain her miscarriage was just a horrible misfortune that would someday reveal a greater purpose. So they tried. And tried. And tried some more to make a baby . . . Nothing.

L.T. returned to football with a vengeance. In 2005, he rushed for 1,462 yards, set a team record with 20 touchdowns (third in the league), passed for 3 touchdowns, and was named to the Pro Bowl.

The 2006 season was even better and might well be remembered as the best of his career and perhaps one of the best years for any running back in NFL history.

Tomlinson rushed for 1,815 yards and set NFL single-season records for most rushing touchdowns (28) and most total touchdowns (31). He also set the NFL record for most points in a season (186), breaking Green Bay Packers great Paul Hornung's forty-six-year-old mark (176), and he was named the NFL's Most Valuable Player, beating out New Orleans Saints quarterback Drew Brees and Indianapolis Colts quarterback Peyton Manning, with forty-four of the fifty votes cast.

A FATHER'S PAIN, A SON'S ANGUISH, A FAMILY'S LOSS

Because we know that suffering produces perseverance; perseverance, character; and character, hope. And hope does not put us to shame, because God's love has been poured out into our hearts through the Holy Spirit, who has been given to us. (Romans 5:3–5)

L.T. grew up about twenty-five miles south of Waco, Texas, on a settlement known as Tomlinson Hill. His ancestors had worked there as slaves of a farmer named James K. Tomlinson. When President Abraham Lincoln freed the slaves, the family kept the Tomlinson name and stayed on the hill to farm.

L.T.'s father, Oliver Tomlinson, had four boys when he married Loreane Lowe in 1973. LaDainian was born six years later. The family moved to Marlin, Texas, for better opportunities, but the couple eventually split. When one of L.T.'s older half brothers, Charles, was stabbed to death in a fight, Oliver was distraught with grief and left the family.

It was during this time that the Tomlinson boys found God. L.T. was sent to a Christian camp in Missouri during the summer. It was fun, L.T. says, and the principles of faith and Christianity began shaping his perspective on how to live his life. Upon returning to Marlin, the boys encouraged their mother to take them to church; and in due time, with God working in the quiet way He does, Loreane became a pastor with her own congregation.

L.T. enjoyed church, but didn't get serious about Christ until his freshman year in high school at University High School in Waco. He had an older cousin, Ernest Lowe, who was a senior. And LaDainian idolized him. When Ernest was saved that year, it didn't just change his life; it changed the life of his young admirer too. Marlin is a small town where boredom, booze, and girls usually resulted in trouble. But L.T. made a conscious decision not to pursue that life.

"What I leaned on was my sports," Tomlinson says. "I'd say, 'Well, Walter Payton or Emmitt Smith wouldn't be out partying.' In order for me to get where I wanted to go—college and then the NFL—I had to be different from a lot of what was around me. I had to stand out in a different way. And that helped me make good decisions."

Tomlinson wasn't a saint. He's careful to mention that. He tried to do the right things, but as he got older and peer pressure increased, he would "backslide," as his mother put it.

"When you are a kid, you are still learning and evolving as a human being and a man," Tomlinson says. "But my foundation was always my belief in Christ and the teachings of the Bible, and that kept me out of a lot of trouble, especially when I saw my buddies selling drugs or going to jail or joining a gang. I stayed away from those things.

"There are consequences with every choice you make, to our society, but also to God. And He always knows what you are doing," Tomlinson continues. "I remember my mom used to have us read the paper, and she'd point out where somebody our age was getting in trouble and she'd talk about choices and consequences. People my age going to jail; people being killed. And you started to think, *I don't want to be like that. I want to do something great with my life. I want to live like God wants me to live.*"

L.T. met LaTorsha Oakley at a party at Texas Christian University in Waco, Texas. She was a Bill Gates Millennium Scholar and was attending on scholarship. Their first date was at a late-night IHOP near campus, where he spent most of the evening talking about his mother. They were married in 2003.

Faith and family mean so much to L.T. that he has reminders tattooed on his body. He has the initials *LT* on his right arm above an image of God's hands in prayer. He has a University High School Bulldog on his chest. There is a large family tree on his back, and on his shoulder he has the words *My Inspiration* tattooed under a picture of his mother.[1]

LaDainian's father, Oliver, returned home after nearly a decade, and the two reconciled. With the miscarriage of his daughter, LaDainian began to understand how his father must have been affected by the death of his son Charles years earlier, and the two began to get close. It was almost two years to the day of the doctor's visit when L.T. learned his wife had miscarried, that he would be tested again.

On February 23, 2007, L.T.'s half brother, Ronald McClain, was driving their father back to Waco after a trip to the family home on Tomlinson Hill. A tire blew, the truck veered off the road, and Ronald overcorrected, flipping the truck and sending it into a ditch. Oliver, seventy-one, died immediately, and Ronald, forty-eight, died later that afternoon at Waco's Hillcrest Baptist Medical Center.

Things just kept piling up for Tomlinson, a man whom God had given all the blessings of wealth and fame and who appeared to be living the dream life. He'd lost a grandmother in 2004 and an aunt in 2005, LaTorsha had the miscarriage in 2005, and now Oliver and Ronald had died in the truck accident.

"When I lost my father, I was shaken up a bit because we had reached the point where I was just getting to know him good, hanging out and the whole father-son relationship. And I remember thinking, *What's going to happen next?* And for a while, I was definitely in a depressed state and just really sad."

L.T. worked through his grief by staying close to his family

---

1. http://www.magaarchive.tcu.edu/articles/2001-01-CV.asp?issueid=200001.

while training, and he was heavily involved in his Touching Lives Foundation, which promotes education, self-esteem, and cultural self-awareness. He funds programs like a School Is Cool scholarship, a holiday program that gives books and toys to sick kids at Children's Hospital, and a youth football camp and charity golf tournament.

In 2007, Tomlinson led the league in rushing for a second consecutive season with 1,474 yards, moved past Chicago Bears running back Walter Payton on the all-time rushing touchdown list with number 111, and was voted to his fifth Pro Bowl.

In 2008, L.T. fought to overcome toe and groin injuries. After a slow start, he finished the season with 1,110 yards and 11 touchdowns.

He was thirty years old when the 2009 season began. He sprained his ankle during the preseason and was forced to miss the home opener against the Baltimore Ravens. His production declined, and L.T. finished the season with 730 rushing yards and 12 rushing touchdowns.

Four years after learning they had miscarried, L.T. and LaTorsha were still trying to have a baby. In spite of the money and fame, the one thing L.T. wanted more than anything in life was still eluding him. And the couple couldn't understand why. They put their faith in God the day their first child died and were convinced He would make His plan clear and reward them. The couple went back to the doctor for tests. Could there be something wrong with their reproductive systems? Could one of them be sterile? . . . The tests were negative. The doctors said they were in perfect health.

Then a family member asked LaTorsha if she was aware of a medical condition that ran in the family and affected childbearing.

It was like lightning had struck, as though God Himself had cleared His throat and was about to speak. It had been four years since the doctors uttered those five life-altering words: "I can't find the heartbeat." Four years since she sat at the hospital in her husband's arms trying to understand *why*. Four years since they placed their faith in a plan they couldn't understand, but believed someday

He would make clear to them. Four years of lovemaking and no pregnancies.

She returned to the doctor's office and learned that she had Sjogren's syndrome, an autoimmune disease that can cut off the blood supply to a fetus. The good news, they learned, is that it was treatable![2]

Now, if they could just get pregnant. They'd been trying for years—unaware that if LaTorsha had become pregnant before they learned about her condition, there is a chance her subsequent babies would have died too.

A few weeks after learning of his wife's condition, LaDainian arrived at Qualcomm Stadium for a November 15, 2009, matchup with the Philadelphia Eagles. It was a big game because the AFC West division lead was on the line. When LaDainian got to his locker, he found a purple bag with a note: "Please Open Immediately—LaTorsha." He thought it might be a necklace. Instead, he found a pregnancy test kit.

Yep, he was going to be a daddy.

L.T., the father-to-be, rushed for 96 yards and 2 TDs that day to guide the Chargers to a 31–23 victory and into a first-place tie with the Denver Broncos in the AFC West division. If that wasn't enough, he also surpassed former Buffalo Bills running back Thurman Thomas and former Pittsburgh Steelers running back Franco Harris to move into twelfth place on the NFL's all-time career rushing list with 12,145 rushing yards. And his two rushing touchdowns gave him 146 for his career, moving him ahead of former Oakland Raiders running back Marcus Allen and into third place on the all-time list.

"Once we found out about the disease and the injections and what was necessary to keep our baby healthy, everything was golden," Tomlinson says. "That couldn't have been anything other than God that led us here. You can't convince me it wasn't God's plan. The doctors didn't know. They had no idea what was wrong.

---

2. http://articles.nydailynews.com/2010-08-08/sports/27072042_1_/ adainian-tomlinson-baby-girl-moments.

"I started to wonder, 'God, You said it would happen. Are You lying to me?' I was starting to feel like that. That was around the time we started to have the doctors check us and make sure nothing was wrong. At the time, I felt like God was saying, 'Are you losing faith in Me?' and shortly after that it happened and I was like, 'OK, God, I'm sorry. You had a plan. I started to wonder when we couldn't get pregnant. You had a plan. What was I thinking?'

"He didn't let us get pregnant until we learned what to do so the baby would be healthy," Tomlinson says. "We tried for years and started to doubt a little, and then as soon as we found out what the problem was and there was a solution for it, we got pregnant right away. That's not part of God's plan? Of course it was. There was a plan all along. It's hard not to question and wonder. But it goes to show there is a reason for everything."

Tomlinson was released from the Chargers on February 22, 2010, exactly five years to the day after he learned of LaTorsha's miscarriage. In March of that year, he signed a two-year free agent contract with the New York Jets and would play a significant role that season, rushing for 914 yards and 6 touchdowns.

LaTorsha's labor was induced on July 7, 2010. Doctors pulled out the head, and then showed LaDainian how to pull out the rest of the baby. In one big swoosh, Daylen Oliver Tomlinson burst through the line. His stats: 7 pounds, 1 ounce, 20 inches.

By January 2011, LaTorsha was pregnant again. The couple had their second child, a daughter named Dayah Lynn Tomlinson, on September 10, 2011. She was 6 pounds, 12 ounces, and 19 inches long. After spending the night sleeping on a bench at the hospital, Daddy drove to MetLife Stadium for the Jets' Sunday night season opener against the Dallas Cowboys.[3] In his new role as a third-down back,

3. http://www.nydailynews.com/blogs/jets/2011/09/ladainian-tomlinson-becomes-father-sleeps-on-hospital-bench-night-before-season-opening.

he rushed 5 times for 16 yards and led the team with 6 receptions for 73 yards in the Jets' 27–24 victory.

L.T., nearing retirement, says he is growing the family he and LaTorsha always dreamed of. And when they are old enough, he will tell them about the lesson his Lord and Savior taught him during the most difficult stretch in his life and of the great reward he received for his patience and trust in God.

5

TEMPTATION

The acts of the flesh are obvious: sexual immorality, impurity and debauchery; idolatry and witchcraft; hatred, discord, jealousy, fits of rage, selfish ambition, dissensions, factions and envy; drunkenness, orgies, and the like. I warn you, as I did before, that those who live like this will not inherit the kingdom of God

—Galatians 5:19–21

Attractive young women send NFL players nude photos with offers of free sex. Others hang out in hotel lobbies waiting for the team buses to arrive so they can present themselves and a girlfriend for a group party. And then there are the crazies, who try to climb into players' dorm windows during training camp or call them at home during dinner with their families.

The Bible is filled with examples of men who have been felled by women: Eve tempted Adam into betraying God by eating the forbidden fruit. Delilah wooed Samson into cutting his locks. And David committed adultery with the beautiful Bathsheba, then sent her husband into battle to be killed.

Sex has been man's downfall throughout time and will likely

be the downfall of our sons and grandsons and great-grandsons. No doubt, we are often our own worst enemies, eagerly engaging in sex acts and calling ourselves "lucky."

Sexual temptations are bad enough for ordinary men, with ordinary looks, ordinary talents, and ordinary wealth. But it's far worse for celebrities. Women are drawn to money, power, and fame. And men spend lifetimes trying to acquire those measures of success to secure a woman's love.

NFL coaches, players, and chaplains agree that of all the temptations that can derail a promising athlete, sex is the hands-down winner. Gambling, alcohol, steroids, recreational drugs, bad friends—they all trail sex by a mile.

New York Giants defensive end Justin Tuck says he watches teammates hounded by women who are so beautiful and shapely, ordinary men can't get a "hello," let alone a date. He knows the pitfalls and offers this cold, hard truth to rookies and other new arrivals to the Giants' locker room.

"I tell them, 'It's probably not because you're handsome,'" Tuck says. "They want to get pregnant."

The average NFL salary in 2011 was $2.25 million, with rookies guaranteed a minimum of $375,000, according to the NFL union. No more than 3 percent of that can go to the agent, another 40 percent goes to taxes, and the part that's left over is what makes that 320-pound defensive tackle, with the protruding belly and persistent snoring, one of the sexiest men alive.

No man is immune. The most ardent Christian can fall. God is clear where He stands on sleeping around. Sexual immorality is addressed in numerous Bible scriptures.

First Corinthians 6:18 urges, "Flee from sexual immorality. All other sins a person commits are outside the body, but whoever sins sexually, sins against their own body."

In 1 Thessalonians 4:3–5, Paul wrote, "It is God's will that you should be sanctified: that you should avoid sexual immorality; that each of you should learn to control your own body in a way that is holy and honorable, not in passionate lust like the pagans, who do not know God."

And in Exodus 20:14, 17, God's seventh and tenth commandments read: "You shall not commit adultery. . . . You shall not covet your neighbor's house. You shall not covet your neighbor's wife, or his male or female servant, his ox or donkey, or anything that belongs to your neighbor."

Practically speaking, it leads to diseases and can undermine the family structure. And yet, players still find themselves lured into meaningless, loveless sexual encounters with women in ways that undermine their physical and emotional health, their financial security, and in some cases, the longevity of their NFL careers.

Tuck had been married four years and had a baby when the 2011 season began. He had sex before marriage and has told friends and teammates that he regrets it.

"To this day I wish I could take it back," he says. "My wife was a virgin before we married, and I wasn't. Just knowing that I could have saved myself for her, and there would have been nothing impure about it . . . I wish I could go back."

NFL locker rooms are a place where anything and everything is discussed in the open. It's not uncommon to hear players talk about their dates and sexual adventures in explicit detail. And the stories, if believable, can be mesmerizing.

But there is also a small, perhaps less vocal group of players who say sex is overhyped and plays too great a role in a player's notion of self-worth.

Tuck says he's had many discussions with teammates, both Christian and non-Christian, who have concluded that sex isn't the end-all and be-all that it's perceived to be on television or when a good storyteller is spinning his yarn.

"I've had guys say to me, 'It's not as macho as you think it is,'" Tuck says. "Once you hit twenty-eight, twenty-nine, thirty years old, you start to realize that it's just a false pretense. The idea that the more girls you sleep with, the bigger the man you are—it's not the case. I don't have any profound way of saying it, but I tell the guys the honest truth about it."

Washington Redskins safety Oshiomogho Atogwe says pre-marital sex amounts to "trading future glories for temporary pleasures. "You are looking for something exciting and fun, but what you are giving up is worth so much more," he says. "When you haven't known anybody, that's way more precious when you grow with each other [in marriage] without the excess baggage. That's so much more valuable than those times when you had some fun. To me, the witness of staying pure speaks a lot more loudly than almost anything else man-to-man because it's man's biggest struggle."

It's ironic, Tuck says. He'll sometimes see young players emerging as great talents on the field, but in their private lives, they are so desperate to be accepted by their teammates and friends that they'll do whatever makes them popular no matter the consequences.

Sometimes that means sleeping with a woman to share a story and be one of the guys. Other times, it might mean getting a tattoo.

"It used to be cool," Tuck admits. "You'd say, 'Oh, that's a cool tattoo.' But now everyone has one. I think it's cool when guys don't have tattoos because it means they didn't fall into that trap of 'I'm going to do something because everyone else is doing it.'

"I'm going to be my own person. I'm going to be me. Of course, that's easier said than done. But that's why it's a show of strength and leadership.

"We all know that you are supposed to remain pure before marriage, and I think if you have the strength to do it, it shows something special about a person," Tuck acknowledges. "It shows that you are a bigger man and can resist temptation."

To be fair, saying no to sex gets easier with age. The drive subsides, we become more disciplined and better at weighing the risk versus the reward, we have spouses to take care of our needs, and frankly there are fewer women who want to have sex with us.

It's much harder to say no when you are a teenager and you're the only virgin in the locker room. No one wants to be the geek—or at least, to admit to it.

"It's tough facing it when you are a teenage boy or a college boy because it's the uncool thing," Atogwe says. "Everyone is so interested in being among the popular crowd or cool crowd, and this is definitely the uncool thing. But it's not like you are going to lose your friends over it."

Atogwe says even though he's a married adult, he still faces some of the peer pressure and uncomfortable situations that teenagers do. He plays with rookies who are sleeping around and veterans who are running around on their wives, which he disapproves of. And he still has to share a locker room and have interpersonal relationships with them. This is no different from non-football players who share office space and have to listen to their co-workers' "glory" stories on Monday mornings.

Atogwe decided that while he can still be their friend and teammate, he just can't get involved in some of their activities. So maybe that means he doesn't go out with them on Friday night.

"I can't go out with you because I know what living like that, how that offends God, and I know how that is going to affect your life going forward," Atogwe says. "I am your friend, and I'll share with you and laugh with you and love you. And I'll do anything I can to help you if you need me. But I just can't go there with you."

God isn't cruel. He doesn't give us sexual urges and then ask us to deny them. He gives us a wonderful opportunity to explore our sexuality with great joy and wonderment. What He asks is that we do it in a committed relationship rather than in frivolous encounters with groupies and other women who have their own agendas.

First Corinthians 7:1–9 says:

"It is good for a man not to have sexual relations with a woman." But since sexual immorality is occurring, each man should have sexual relations with his own wife, and each woman with her own husband. The husband should fulfill his marital duty to his wife, and likewise the wife to her husband. The wife does not have authority over her own body but yields it to her husband. In the same way, the husband does not have authority over his own body but yields it to his wife. Do not deprive each other except perhaps by mutual consent and for a time, so that you may devote yourselves to prayer. Then come together again so that Satan will not tempt you because of your lack of self-control. I say this as a concession, not as a command. I wish that all of you were as I am. But each of you has your own gift from God; one has this gift, another has that.

Now to the unmarried and the widows I say: It is good for them to stay unmarried, as I do. But if they cannot control themselves, they should marry, for it is better to marry than to burn with passion.

While the passage makes it clear that it's who we sleep with, rather than how much sex we have, the point seems to be lost on many players as they jump from one bed to the next as proof of their high social status and desirability or for their own momentary physical pleasure.

Tuck has seen his share of the celebrity life. He's had women try to crawl in his windows at camp, and he once watched a woman leave a teammate's room after sex and then walk down the hall and knock on his door for a second go of it.

"That's when you know she is just trying to get pregnant. It's the money, no question," he says. "Those girls are with you because of what you do and what you can provide. But when your career ends and the money stops coming in and their lifestyle has to change, that's when you wind up divorced. If they marry you for the money, once the money stops, what's keeping them attracted anymore? Like I said, it's probably not your looks."

Washington Redskins chaplain Brett Fuller said sex is one of the most popular discussion topics among players at Bible study because it's such a big part of a man's life and a player's celebrity. Even players who truly want to stay pure struggle with the smorgasbord of sexual offerings.

"It's not just at training camp," Fuller says. "It's at the gas station; it's when they are at the grocery store; it's all the time."

Here's what he tells his players:

"Number one, the young lady who is doing it probably doesn't have the purest of thoughts. They want something more than your love; be very careful and wise.

"Second, I realize it is a lot of fun. But practically speaking, there are a number of diseases you can get, and it's not likely that you are the only man this woman is sleeping with. A monogamous relationship is important.

"Three, you are called by God as a man that is saved for one woman and her for you. Don't spoil it by spreading yourself so thin that you see somebody else's face on your wife. Save yourself. I promise you, it's worth it. There is value in being pure.

"Lastly, rather than looking for the person who is Mrs. Right, you become Mr. Right. You don't want to marry a woman who has been sleeping around with everybody—why in the world would a woman want to marry a man who has been sleeping around with everybody? Concentrate on being Mr. Right and I promise you, you will build a foundation for your marriage that starts while you are single."

Tennessee Titans quarterback Matt Hasselbeck has a beautiful, athletic wife whom he fell in love with almost from the time he met her during their freshman year at Boston College. He speaks of her glowingly and then pauses to acknowledge that under the right circumstances, any man can slip and fall, ruining his marriage, his family, and his life.

From his first year in the NFL, Hasselbeck surrounded himself with teammates who would hold him accountable and be a friend if he was ever in need of one.

"Sex is a temptation all the time, and it lasts your entire lifetime," he admits. "Where you hang out and who you surround yourself with are really important in avoiding trouble.

"I have so many friends that are really solid guys, and they have slipped and fallen. I guess the lesson is, if you think you are too righteous to slip, then you have been fooled. It can happen to anybody."

Hasselbeck remembers his first year in the league with the Green Bay Packers. He'd gone to a Bible study during training camp, and it was packed. Players are often scared they are going to get injured or cut from the squad, so training camp is a time when everyone gets religious.

That first night, Pro Bowl defensive end Reggie White, the team's most devout Christian, said he had a few words he wanted to share with the Bible study, so the team chaplain gave him the floor.

He wanted to talk about the women who would be descending on camp and how he personally handled it when a woman approached him.

"He would say something like, 'I'm sorry, I'm married. I do not want to talk to you. Get away from me,'" says Hasselbeck.

"I was like, 'Come on. That's so extreme.' But he said it was a risk-reward thing. He was like, 'No. I'm going to draw the line right *here*.'

"He was saying that if you draw a line right here and then stand right next to it, if something goes wrong, it will be easy to fall over the line.

"But if you draw a line and then stand back ten yards and something goes wrong and you fall, well, now you are nowhere near the line."

In other words, there is no reason to walk right up to temptation. Keep some distance. If you talk to enough women at a bar or club, whether it's just a friendly conversation or not, you are more likely to succumb. Every single guy gets needy. Every married man goes through tough stretches with his wife and romanticizes the good times before he got married and was a chick magnet.

But Hasselbeck says it goes beyond sleeping around. Even the hint of infidelity or flirting can be damaging to his marriage, his reputation, and his family.

Take, for example, fan photographs.

"Everyone wants to get their picture taken or an autograph. And that's great," he says. "But I'm conservative about what I sign or where I sign it. Some people want to get real close, and I'm careful about where my hands are and what my body language is.

"Ask yourself: What if this goes on the Internet? How is this going to make my wife feel? Say it's some girl, her child, and me in the photo. I'm like, 'Oh, hey, let's throw the husband in too,' or let's make sure the body language is appropriate for the situation. But then sometimes you notice how she is standing, and it's like, 'Oh, what is the right thing to do and then click. The shot is taken.'"

Hasselbeck met his wife, Sarah, when he was a seventeen-year-old freshman at Boston College. They dated through college with one two-week break and later a semester break. He wed at twenty-four, and the couple now has three children.

Married eleven years when the 2011 season began, the Hasselbecks had built up a certain amount of trust. But Hasselbeck says that can be a pitfall for couples who depend on it too much.

"The number one need for a woman is to feel loved, and that's one reason a woman needs to hear 'I love you,' 'I love you,' 'I love you," he shares. "As a guy, you are sitting there thinking, *You know I love you. I'm sitting here on the couch next to you. I married you. What more do you need?*

"But they are naturally drawn to wanting the security of being loved unconditionally forever and knowing it's not going to change. It doesn't matter who you are or how much trust you've built up; it's one of those things that has to be priority number one."

Hasselbeck said it's not the obvious mistakes he's worried about. If a woman were to approach him and offer him a sexual favor in her car, he'll quickly blow her off and move on. Instead, he's concerned about the ones that are more subtle. The ones where the woman seems like just a friend, and a little at a time she asks more and more of a player until the athlete suddenly realizes he's developing feelings. Hasselbeck says players, and probably men in general, get in trouble when they start rationalizing the relationship or the meetings with the woman—it was a friendly lunch, just a friendly kiss, just a back rub—until you guiltily tell a friend or your wife, "We weren't doing anything." By then, it's already gone too far.

Hasselbeck is a veteran, so when he travels he isn't required to have a roommate like he did as a rookie. But he has one anyway. He says that he's never planned on cheating on Sarah, but with another person in the room, he knows nothing is going to happen, and it probably makes it a non-issue for Sarah and the kids too.

"If my kids ask, 'Where's Dad tonight?' [Sarah] can say he and Mr. Whoever are in St. Louis. They share a room. 'Oh, OK.' There is security in that," he says. "And that's true with the temptation to use a remote control or view things on a laptop too. It's you and another Christian guy, where your morals and values during the day are the same as they are at night, and you both have accountability."

Temptation doesn't always come in a glitzy night club, a dark secluded meeting place, or an Internet chat room.

Sometimes, it's in broad daylight, when a player's wife is

standing right next to him. Or when he's playing with his kids at training camp. Or when he's picking up a gallon of milk from the grocery store.

NFL players' wives know the groupies are all over town. They are married and single, they are very young and very old, they make passes at the players day and night, and they do it whether his wife is standing next to him or is nowhere in sight.

Cabrina Womack, wife of Arizona Cardinals offensive guard Floyd Womack, says wives look out for one another and close ranks when groupies appear at player functions.

"Some women will approach the girl and say, 'Who are you here for? Who is your man?' The wives are very cliquey and protective of their husbands. So if we see a groupie, we give them the side eye. We try to make them feel uncomfortable," she says.

"When you see a girl just kind of standing there, you are automatically like, 'Well, we're going to go over and see who she is.' Maybe she's going to say, 'I'm such and such's girlfriend or wife, but if you don't have an answer, you are getting the side eye, the nasty names. They just don't tolerate it. It's almost like a wives' code. If I have a girlfriend, I don't bring her to functions. You just don't do that. You don't bring a single girlfriend to a function around other players and other players' wives. That's unacceptable."

Danisha Rolle, wife of former Baltimore Ravens cornerback Samari Rolle, says some of the fooling around comes out of a frustration with marriage itself and the misunderstanding men and women have about how their roles and relationships change when they transition from boyfriend/girlfriend to husband/wife. It's not just an "athlete" problem, she says; it's a "people" problem, no matter their profession, wealth, or talent. It's just heightened for players because of their celebrity.

It's like this: After years of being told he's the greatest player to come out of his hometown, he starts dating. And during the courtship, the woman is trying to impress, attract, and win over her future husband. She squeezes his muscles and tells him how strong he is. She pulls out pictures from a party and tells him how handsome he is. She talks to him late at night after a round of passionate lovemaking and tells him what a wonderful lover he is.

Then they get married.

Suddenly, ole handsome farts, snores, and thinks taking out the trash is beneath him. The friendships he once enjoyed with other women and the chitchat with a pretty girl in an autograph line or at the agent's office look suspicious and get nixed by the wife. And the wild, adventurous sex in the car, in the woods, on the kitchen table is . . . unbecoming of a married woman.

"When you are dating, you're being courted," Danisha says. "That's when you are still in that honeymoon phase where he's lingering on your every word or sentence. You're being attentive and caring, and it isn't until you are married and you relax and you feel like, 'I got you now.' It's not always that obvious, but it's subconscious. The date nights you used to schedule lessen, and the day-to-day takes over."

If you are married, you get it. If you are single, no matter how many warnings you receive, you won't believe it until you are married. That's just one of life's truths. But one thing is certain, chaplains say: if you have chosen the right spouse and are committed to walking with God through eternity, these are small sacrifices for a lifetime of companionship and love.

WALKING THE WALK

Corwin Anthony, a former NFL tight end and Miami Dolphins chaplain, joined Athletes in Action in 2000 and became the pro ministry director in 2006.

As a player and chaplain, he's known athletes who have taken advantage of their celebrity to sleep with multitudes of women. And the one thing he's learned is that no matter how much sex a player gets, his cup is never full.

"There were so many guys who you would observe from a distance and say, 'He's got the money, the babes, the fame, and all the parties he can go to. Wow.' And then we'd sit down and talk privately in a one-on-one situation, and I'd hear: 'I'm lonely. I'm miserable. I have no real friends. I'm addicted to sex.' . . . . I'd hear this from the star players; guys who were at the top of their games and really riding high with everything a young man could desire," Anthony says.

Anthony would respond by sharing the Word of God and talking to them about changing their lifestyle. But sometimes, a guy just isn't ready to change.

Anthony's grandfather, Rev. Lee Anthony, was a pastor, and Corwin heard the Scripture from a young age. He understood Christianity, but like most young men, he wasn't terribly committed. As an athlete, he had pretty girls readily available to him. And once he enrolled at UCLA and got away from family, there were just too many good times to be had.

In 1987, he met UCLA's team chaplain, Mike Bunkley, who challenged him to change his life. Anthony was feeling the urge to return to his Christian roots, but wasn't ready to give up the parties or the sex. Inside, he was in turmoil. Like many of his charges today, he started ducking the chaplain.

"The commandments that God gives us are not meant to keep us from having fun, but to protect us and provide for us," he says. "But it was the sex that was one of the biggest reasons I didn't want to fully commit to Christ."

There's not a man on earth who doesn't understand exactly what Anthony was going through. Some might say that he hadn't gotten his fill or sown his oats. There was some part of him that needed to feel he'd gotten "enough" to make him feel like a man.

Very few men attending a university with thousands of available young women look over the quad as they are heading to class and think, *I only want to be with* one *of them.*

This is why team chaplains like Anthony—especially those who have played the game and walked the walk—are able to make an impression on today's players. They understand the significance of asking a young man to give up free sex and adoration for an even more satisfying walk with God.

It's one thing to take the high road and refrain from sleeping around if you are Jimbo at the grocery store and no one wants to sleep with you. It's quite another to refrain from enjoying multiple partners if everywhere you go, women want to have sex, and they are all saying it's "OK, just for fun, no strings attached."

If a player seems receptive, but still hasn't bought Anthony's sales pitch about self-sacrifice and the godly life, he tells the player the story of a pretty, young gymnast named Kim Hamilton, whom he met in college and started dating.

She'd overcome poverty and her father's drug addiction to become a four-time NCAA gymnastics champion, a six-time All-American, and a UCLA Hall of Fame inductee. Her book, *Unfavorable Odds*, took ten years to write and is definitely worth a read.

"I had my eye on her for over a year," Anthony tells his athletes. "I'd committed my life to Christ and was reading and studying my Bible, and then we started dating. And I'm thinking, *God, this is not fair. I'm trying to live free, and You finally put this girl in front of me.* . . . So I hid my faith from her because I was afraid that if I acted too much like a Christian, she'd leave me."

The relationship became intimate, and Anthony was overcome with guilt. He was struggling to live a double life: praying and preaching about God's hopes for our salvation in one moment, and then making love to his girlfriend the next.

One day, he just sat up in bed and said to her: "I have to stop . . . I have to stop having sex." Corwin explained to Kim that while God wants us to enjoy all the pleasure that comes from sex, He wants us to do it within the context of marriage. So they decided to abstain.

Their hearts were in the right place, but they found it difficult not to backslide. "We'll just kiss" never works, he says. And so they went through good periods and bad periods and periods where they just gave up and went at it.

Their battle with sexual impurity weighed on them, and the couple would break up and then get back together. In time, Corwin and Kim found one another, and they have now been in a loving marriage for more than twenty years.

"Every young person is in the process of growing and learning what it means to be with God and to have Him in their lives," Anthony says. "Naturally, you don't get it right at first. I look back at myself when I first committed my life to Christ and my life did not change overnight. I was still making mistakes, but I was also growing and learning, and that's part of it. So, I understand what the players are going through, and while I sympathize, I'm going to tell them the truth."

FAME NEVER AGES

It's not just the players.

Minnesota Vikings coach Leslie Frazier, now in his fifties, is married and has three children, including a son who plays defensive back at Rice University. Frazier, who played defensive back for the Chicago Bears from 1981 to 1986 and has spent the past two decades coaching at the college and professional ranks, says women a generation younger still approach him when they learn he is a former player and now an NFL coach.

"It doesn't matter whether you come from New York City or Podunk U; people want to be around celebrity, which is why reality TV is so big today," Frazier says. "If they can be associated with celebrity, it kind of gives them status and improves their self-worth or self-image in their own minds, so that sometimes causes girls to gravitate to you. It's not because you are a handsome guy, but because you can intercept passes, score points, or throw touchdowns. It's your celebrity. And maybe one day you are going to be a rich guy along with being famous."

Frazier said most people assume players are tempted the most during the NFL season, but that's not true. Players are most likely to find trouble in the off-season, when they lack the structure that comes with attending practice and team activities and they find themselves with lots of free time and money to spend. It's worse on younger players who are still immature and usually don't have family obligations or marital relationships to keep them grounded.

Frazier remembers former Bears like Vince Evans, Roland Harper, and Al Harris pulling younger players like him, Mike Singletary, and Jeff Fisher aside to talk about their lifestyle away from Halas Hall and to discuss how they should handle themselves in different environments. "I took it to heart," Frazier says. "One of the things they impressed upon me is, 'Don't try and do it alone. You need to get plugged into a church. You need to get plugged into a small group.' What they were saying is that if you get out on an island by yourself, the temptation is so overwhelming, you are going to fall prey to it. You are still human. You still have the same desires that any other man does, you know?"

Shortly after he joined the Bears, Frazier, who was one of the starting cornerbacks when Chicago won Super Bowl XX, would oftentimes be approached by a friend, or a friend of a friend, who would ask him to come to a party. His notoriety as a Bears player would be great for the gathering because it would encourage more people to show up—especially women. "Well, I am twenty-two, twenty-three years old," Frazier says, reflecting on those days. "If I show up at that party and some girl starts hitting on me, it's going to be hard to get in my car and drive home, you know? So what I tried to do is avoid those kinds of situations as best I could. I might say, 'I'll see if I can make it,' knowing that I wouldn't because if I showed up, I'd fall prey to that temptation."

CHILD CELEBRITIES

The battle doesn't stop with the players and coaches. Anyone who has seen reality television in recent years knows how dad's wealth and celebrity can make the kids just as popular (and vulnerable) to the high school sex and party scene. It's about status, albeit, unearned, that makes them the cool kid whose dad played or coached in the NFL.

The fathers aren't stupid. They know this. In fact, NFL fathers who have been exposed to NFL groupies might be the hardest dads in the world to fool.

Jeff Saturday, the longtime Indianapolis Colts center who signed a two-year free agent contract with the Green Bay Packers this off-season, has eleven- and five-year-old sons and a nine-year-old daughter. He says he'll keep the sex conversations practical rather than getting too heavy into religion.

"When you're fourteen and you are with a girl who's telling you she'll do anything you want, that's tough," he says. "Every man who isn't a believer will tell you this is something you should do. This is what makes you a man. That's not true.

"You can't put yourself in a position where you know you are going to fail. Once you are on the couch in the dark, pants coming off, it's really too late. You have to make this decision on your own, and it has to have a conviction deep inside you."

Mike Singletary, whose youngest son was thirteen and his oldest twenty-three in the fall of 2011, took a different approach.

"I told my sons that the most important thing is that we want to honor God with our lives," Singletary shares. "Before you go anywhere and do anything, make sure you have your mind made up.

Don't go somewhere and 'What if this woman comes up? Maybe if she's a blonde. Maybe if she's tall. Maybe if . . .' No. You know what? It's no. I'm not going to compromise. I have to answer to God.

"I want my sons to be men of honor, and I tell them about the mistakes I made because no one talked to me about those things, and I just tell them the truth."

Denver Broncos safety Brian Dawkins played in his ninth Pro Bowl following the 2011 season, placing him in a tie with former Tampa Bay safety John Lynch for second most Pro Bowls at the position, one behind former Washington Redskins safety Ken Houston.

Dawkins says talking only goes so far. Kids get tired of lectures. He's depending on his kids seeing how he treats one very important woman every day to guide their behavior.

"It's not so much what I say to them; it's more that they see how I treat their mother every day," Dawkins says. "I want to be a reflection of the proper way to treat women. I know the temptation is going to come; it's only natural that they'll start looking at girls in that way. But I want them to see the women as someone's sister and mother instead of as an object. Once they start seeing them as an object to have or take, that's when they get in trouble."

6

TO LOVE ONE ANOTHER

A new command I give you: Love one another. As I have loved you, so you must love one another. By this everyone will know that you are my disciples, if you love one another.

—John 13:34–35

Football teams are like companies. Employees come from various economic, cultural, and religious backgrounds. Good football coaches, like good managers, must be able to communicate and motivate all their workers. To put this cultural divide into perspective, consider that the NFL started the 2011 season with roughly nineteen hundred players ages twenty to forty-two, with educations ranging from high school to graduate school and with salaries beginning at the NFL rookie minimum $375,000 and rising as high as the average $18 million a year that New England Patriots quarterback Tom Brady and Indianapolis Colts quarterback Peyton Manning were paid. It's a diverse group. And if coaches are going to be effective at reaching out to all their young men, they need to respect the players' individuality. And that includes who they place their faith in, whether it is Jesus Christ, Allah, or some other religious figure.

Former Minnesota Vikings coach Brad Childress, 39-35 in nearly five seasons with the Vikings, was one of the most religious head coaches in pro football until he was fired in November 2010 after the team fell to 3-7.

He'd made news a year earlier when he demonstrated that respect for people of other religions by accommodating Husain Abdullah, a Muslim who practiced his faith with great devotion.

The then second-year player out of Washington State was an up-and-coming safety who had developed a reputation as one of the Vikings' best special-teams players. Coaches say he had a penchant for hard work and flying to the ball, which is why Childress was perplexed when Abdullah looked sluggish during the team's 2009 training camp. What the coach didn't realize was that Muslims had begun Ramadan, the holiest month in the Muslim calendar. During this time, Muslims seek spiritual purification through fasting from sunrise to sunset, abstaining from sex, and spending time in prayer. Abdullah wasn't eating or drinking during the team's ninety-degree workouts, and his play was being affected. Once Childress learned that Abdullah was abstaining from food and water, he pulled him aside for a question-and-answer session on the Muslim faith and Ramadan.

"I didn't tell anybody because I didn't want any special treatment," explains Abdullah, who has been in the starting lineup since the 2010 season. Childress could see how serious Abdullah was about his faith and knew he had to respect the player's beliefs, just as he wanted others to respect his own Christian values. Childress told Abdullah he would assist the player with his worship and arranged a meeting with the team's nutritional consultant. "I wasn't surprised that he was willing to work with me," Abdullah says. "But I definitely respected him and the Vikings organization for helping me during the month of Ramadan. It meant a lot to me on a personal level."

For the past three summers, during the month of Ramadan, the team has provided Abdullah with a big breakfast before sunrise and a hearty meal after sunset. At 2:00 a.m., Abdullah awakes to drink a protein and carbohydrate milkshake with about four hundred calories and then goes back to sleep. "You would ordinarily eat breakfast, lunch, and dinner. And I just substitute this late meal for lunch," Abdullah says. As long as the heat doesn't become too overwhelming, this regimen enables him to stay hydrated and maintain his 204-pound playing weight. That wasn't always the case for his older brother, Arizona Cardinals' safety Hamza Abdullah, who had broken his fast several times after he was overcome with dehydration in the high desert heat. For the Abdullah family, Ramadan has been a time of celebration since the children were as young as seven.

Abdullah's parents, Sa'eeda and Yusuf, started life as Christians, but converted to Islam in young adulthood, raising Husain and his seven brothers and four sisters as Muslim from birth. In the locker room, Abdullah has a reputation as a soft-spoken, highly intelligent player who befriends teammates regardless of their backgrounds. Much like in the non-football world, he's the kind of person who employers try and accommodate because they are considerate of co-workers and are "good locker-room guys," Childress says. In the early fall of 2011, Abdullah was the father of a four-year-old son, Jalaal, and a two-year-old daughter named Kameela. Like most young fathers, Abdullah thought about the world his children would grow to inherit and wondered why so many wars had been fought because people of different faiths refused to accept and love one another. In NFL locker rooms, acceptance comes from having raw talent, a teammate's trust, and respect for the skills of co-workers and competitors alike.

"The three biggest religions are Islam, Christianity, and Judaism, and all three teach peace, caring for one another, and love," Abdullah shares during a lunch break at the team's Eden Prairie training facility. "If everybody's really practicing the core beliefs of their own religion, we should be able to live together with respect and love for one another. Shouldn't we?"

Muslims are called to prayer five times a day. The noon prayer and the midday prayer, at about 4:00 p.m., usually conflict with a Muslim's work responsibilities whether he's employed by an engineering firm or one of the NFL's thirty-two teams. Rather than be disruptive and ask for a special room to make his prayers during the team's practice or film study, Abdullah waits until he gets home and he makes up for the missed prayers earlier in the day. His teammates and coaches have accepted him, partly because he hasn't put his faith ahead of the team, used his beliefs to seek favors from the organization, or begun preaching in the locker room.

"If you believe in something strongly, people will generally respect you for that even if they don't share those beliefs," Abdullah says. "You are supposed to spread the word. But your job is never to convert anybody; it's just to convey the message. The best way to do that is through personal example because they look at you, and they think, *Oh, he's a pretty stand-up guy,* and they ask you a question about your faith."

It's the same way most Christians handle themselves in NFL locker rooms, players and chaplains say. "If you go around trying to force-feed it to everybody," Abdullah explains, "you're going to get that response: 'Hey man, back up some.' So if anyone has questions for me, they are welcome to ask. But I'm not going around and asking every person in the locker room if they want a copy of the Koran. I have them if they want one, but I'm not going to force it on anyone."

Abdullah is in the minority in this locker room and every other locker room in the league. There are far more Christians than Muslims, Jews, Buddhists, you name the religion. Some years, there are no more than a handful of players actively practicing any faith other than Christianity, chaplains and players say. Abdullah says that he's a devoted Muslim, but that players of any faith tend to be better teammates and co-workers, an opinion that is seconded by many current and former coaches.

"I think people knowing that one day we're all going to die, and that we'll have to answer for our sins, makes us more aware of doing wrong," Abdullah says, while teammates around him are spending their lunch break playing card games, singing along to music on their iPods, and talking to friends and family on their cell phones.

"I think that even those people who don't seem to care on the outside and do whatever moves them . . . if they were raised to believe in God, it's still inside of them. And in the back of their minds they are feeling like, 'I have to answer for this.' And those people are going to be a little more cautious, a little kinder to other people. In the grand scheme, knowing that you will someday have to answer for your actions, I believe, makes you a better teammate, a better co-worker, a better classmate. Life is a struggle, and no one is perfect, regardless of your beliefs. People try to put others on a pedestal too much. Everybody is just a normal person, and we all have our problems that we're trying to work through."

Childress saw the diversity in his locker room and chose to embrace it, something Leslie Frazier, the Vikings assistant chosen to replace him as head coach, has repeated since getting the top job. Accepting others who don't share one's faith or social values isn't always easy, as any worker in America can attest. Like Tony Dungy says in chapter 1, you can't build an all-Christian team—or company for that matter. And that means finding a way to work alongside, or even in a reporting role to, co-workers and managers who have different beliefs. Sometimes, people can be so rigid, even extreme, in their desire that everyone else live and believe as they do, that it can poison the work environment.

The Bible says God loves all of us so much that He sent His only Son to die on the cross for our sins. The emphasis here is the word *all*.

In Luke 9:51–56, Jesus is traveling to Jerusalem in the final days of His earthly life. See how He responded to villagers who either didn't know Him or assumed the worst of His party:

As the time approached for him to be taken up to heaven, Jesus resolutely set out for Jerusalem. And he sent messengers on ahead, who went into a Samaritan village to get things ready for him; but the people there did not welcome him, because he was heading for Jerusalem. When the disciples James and John saw this, they asked, "Lord, do you want us to call fire down from heaven to destroy them?" But Jesus turned and rebuked them. Then he and his disciples went to another village.

Days later, Jesus is being taken to the cross . . .

Two other men, both criminals, were also led out with him to be executed. When they came to the place called the Skull, they crucified him there, along with the criminals—one on his right, the other on his left. Jesus said, "Father, forgive them, for they do not know what they are doing." And they divided up his clothes by casting lots. (Luke 23:32–34)

While Christians can sometimes be overly judgmental of certain non-Christians or those Christians deemed "not faithful enough," there are others whom we love and embrace despite their decidedly unchristian behavior. There is nothing more attractive than a guy with a huge personality, who is genuine and true to who he is, and the NFL is filled with these characters—men you admire for their honesty, toughness, talent, and sense of humor, even if the gift giving is the best part of their Christmas celebration.

No one could epitomize this sort of lovable scoundrel more than New York Jets coach Rex Ryan, who for many years has assembled some of the toughest, most aggressive defenses in the league. To say the Jets defense is going to "get after you" is an understatement, and this brash, outspoken head coach isn't afraid to say exactly what's on his mind whether it offends or not. Here is where men of faith have to bend a little and accept the lifestyles, characters, and language of their teammates and coaches if they want to be part of an NFL team.

In the summer of 2010, Ryan's Jets were the subject of Home Box Office's documentary *Hard Knocks*, a cable television series that is given exclusive access to coaches and players during training camp. They conduct private interviews and use miniaturized microphones and cameras that are placed all over the training facility to catch coaches in those private moments when they are making a decision whether to waive a player, and also humorous times, such as when rookies sing their school song or perform imitations of coaches and teammates as part of their training camp initiation. In the summer of 2010, Pro Bowl cornerback Darrelle Revis, arguably the best defensive back in the league the previous season, was holding out for a better deal. Players were interviewed by the media as they showed up for camp, and most everyone was asked about their missing star. One after another, the players danced around the issue, choosing to speak about their hopes for the season, leaving the contract negotiations to the agents and club executives.

The team was called together for a meeting with Ryan that first day of training camp, and in typical Ryan style, the head coach took the issue head-on, addressing the subject everyone was talking about in his own, ahem, colorful way.

"OK, guys let's go ahead and get started," he said as HBO's cameras rolled. "We have one goal as an organization, don't we? And that's to win the Super Bowl. Right? And that's it. How do we get it done? I want to lead the league in wins. That's what I want on offense, lead the league in wins. OK? We straight with that?

"Defense expectations. Look, guys, we don't have Revis in this building right now. Does it matter that Revis is not here? . . . He's pretty ▮▮▮▮ good. [Laughter from the players] He's pretty good. OK, but you know what, guys? It ain't about one guy. It's about leading the league in ▮▮▮▮ wins on defense, isn't it?

"Special teams expectations. I want to lead the league in something. What is it? Wins. How about that? If we play at our best, we will beat every team in this ███████ league playing at their best. So whose shoulders does it fall on? Ours. We affect how this thing turns out, don't we? And it starts with training camp. We gotta have a great ███████ training camp, men. Last year, hey, we were under the radar, and that's a good place to be. ███████ that.

"The best place to be is when expectations are high. Get used to it. It's always going to be that way. And now let's go out and prove everybody right. We know we're better than you. We don't give a ███████ if you know it or not. We don't give a ███████ if you give us your best game. We're going to give you our best game, and we'll beat the ███████ out of you. How's that? Let's go get it."

NFL training camp isn't Bible school. Young men who have dedicated their entire lives to playing a sport are days or weeks away from being told that the dream is over, that they're just not good enough. And though raw, Ryan's language is par for the course at NFL training camp. And his willingness to address the elephant in the room—Revis's holdout—and his direct no-holds-barred way of speaking about his expectations for the season broke the tension right away, and the team roared with laughter. Bad language isn't reserved for NFL locker rooms. It's just as bad in manufacturing plants, Wall Street trading floors, and fire stations. Men of faith can take a stand against bad language, but many let it go. Two of the league's most faithful players, three-time Pro Bowl quarterback Mark Brunell and five-time Pro Bowl running back LaDainian Tomlinson, were in the locker room that day and laughed at Ryan's speech along with their teammates.

Brunell, a devout Christian who started a church in Jacksonville and has given millions to charitable causes, says a man of faith, whether in the NFL or the local Home Depot, has to pick his battles.

"I'm not going to tell Rex to watch his mouth," Brunell shares during an interview at his New Jersey residence during the summer of 2011. "The only thing that really gets me is when guys use the 'Jesus Christs' and the 'God damns.' When I'm around people I know,

I'll say, 'Hey, come on. Is that necessary?' It doesn't mean they'll stop or change their behavior permanently, but 99.9 percent of the time they usually stop and are like, 'You're right, you're right, yeah, I need to stop that.' But you don't do that with an F-bomb. It's offensive, but it's used so much and isn't directly attacking our faith that I think that would be crossing the line to call them on it. I think using the Lord's name in vain crosses the line, and I think everybody—whether they use those terms or not—would agree with that. And that's the only thing that kind of rubs me wrong. I mean, that's Jesus and that's my guy and you just can't use His name in vain. Don't go there."

Brunell says it's not just curse words or taking the Lord's name in vain that he has to accept as part of the NFL experience. The culture off the football field invariably finds its way into the NFL locker room through popular music, conversations about women, and the culture the players grew up in. Brunell was forty-one in September 2011. His oldest daughter, Caitlin, was attending the University of Alabama and had been a member of the school's Crimson Cabaret dance team the year before. Photos at the Brunell home and on the family's foundation website show a young woman who inherited her mother's good looks, smiling, with her whole life ahead of her. Brunell, however, leaves that loving home and goes to work with a group largely comprised of twentysomething athletes, with superior conditioning, muscular physiques, and all the adulation and sex that come with celebrity. They sit at their lockers moving to the thump-thump-thump of a good beat while rappers use four-letter words to describe what they are going to do to pretty young women like Brunell's daughter. The quarterback might be mature and Christian, but the locker room is filled with players at the polar opposite of Brunell's station in life. And he has to accept that to some degree. The best he can do is to lead by example, he says.

"I'm not a fan of the music," Brunell admits. "That's definitely not something I'm going to miss when my career ends. Being up there in age and being a Christian and having a family, my life is so much different from the lives of my teammates. You hear the music, the four-letter words, the vulgarities, the offensive jokes about women, and I'm not immune to it. I hear it and it still bothers me, but I guess I've gotten used to it after all these years. You can't force your beliefs on other people, especially if they don't want them. I just try and lead by example, and to be approachable. You have to ask yourself how much you are willing to accept and where you draw the line. And that's up to each and every person individually."

Tomlinson shares Brunell's viewpoint. Age and maturity have a lot to do with it. It helps that L.T. has always been something of a homebody whose wife has to drag him out of the house when she needs a little fun. And the couple recently started a family of their own, with two little ones running around their home. L.T., as most fans know him, says that accepting those teammates who don't share his religious or social values in the NFL locker room really isn't all that different from learning to live with your own family.

"Some family members are nonbelievers and you go to a family reunion and you get into this back-and-forth with someone about stuff and what can you do? People are people; you aren't going to kick them out of your family. You still love them. A locker room isn't any different. This is a family, and you have to look out for one another. And you can't pick fights and have a back-and-forth all the time."

Tomlinson admits he didn't always see it this way. He was raised Baptist with a clear sense for right and wrong. Gray wasn't a color or an area in which life was supposed to veer. While discipline and strict guidelines can be good for a child, adults know that life is more complicated, Tomlinson says. Over time, he was able to identify his own flaws, and he learned to be more accepting of flaws in other people. Like Brunell, he's decided to accept others as they are, to reflect long and hard before choosing to take a stand on religious grounds, and to lead by example.

"If I confront everyone, they might be like, 'Jerk, I don't want to hear anything he has to say.' So I roll with it and try to accept people and love them. That's one way my faith has changed," L.T. shares. "I used to believe—being raised as a hard-nosed Baptist—that if you listen to rap music or watch certain shows, you are going to hell. And I've gotten better at accepting people and looking at the long term and trying to be a good example. I want people to be open to me and willing to hear what I have to say, if not now, then later. God's got a plan for their life too. Sometimes you have to back off and let it work and not try and force your beliefs on them. Let God do His thing."

Cleveland Browns pastor Tom Petersburg says he has great hope for the players in his locker room. They can surprise you when you least expect it, he says. Sometimes, the loudest, brashest players who have spent their entire careers seeking the spotlight will show up at a Bible study or reach out to a teammate to ask about his faith. Several chaplains interviewed for this book said one of the most important reasons for pastors to be given locker-room access is so that they can be around and available for players to quietly approach them with a problem or question. Petersburg said that for the most part, players, like kids, are willing to accept one another for who they are and to feel genuine sympathy and care whatever a player's faith or depth of his devotion. This is most evident when a teammate, or even a competitor, is injured in a game. How many times have television cameras shown players taking a knee or holding hands in worship when a stretcher is brought out and a player's head is tied to the board? Everyone waits with bated breath for the player to move a finger or a foot or to give his wife and family a thumbs-up so they know through the television that he is still operating under his own power.

"I had a punter [Reggie Hodges] go down with a torn Achilles in training camp, and he was put on the injured reserve list for the rest of the year," Petersburg says. "Reggie really loves God with all his heart, and everyone knows that. Usually when a player goes down, the coaches just say, 'Move the drill,' and everyone moves to another part of the field. This time they didn't. They all stood there and watched the trainers tend to him, and when they carted him off the field, the team came together and prayed for him—all the coaches and all the players. Reggie has this infectious enthusiasm about Christ in such a way that it doesn't put people off. A lot of people disagree with him, some have responded, others ignore him, but they all respect him so much because he's genuine, the real thing, and that's why that happened on the field."

Several weeks after Childress learned of Abdullah's fasting and took steps to support his player's worship, he noticed a group of players standing near one another in the locker room, and it dawned on him that each man was of a different faith. He thought to himself, *Great teams are built on mutual respect and understanding for every member of the team, all pulling together to accomplish one goal.*

Abdullah was one of the players getting dressed. A second, whom Childress declined to identify, was a Jehovah's Witness, whose religious beliefs wouldn't allow him to take part in an upcoming pregame ceremony recognizing the September 11 attack on the World Trade Center. Jehovah's Witnesses reject much of modern Christianity in favor of what they believe to be a restoration of first-century Christianity. The religion was developed in response to what was perceived to be "compromise and corruption in mainstream Christianity and it repudiates common Christian doctrines such as the Trinity, hellfire and immortality of the soul," according to the *New World Encyclopedia*. As with Abdullah, Childress accepted the player's faith and gave him permission to stand quietly in the stadium tunnel until the ceremony ended before joining his team on the sidelines.

The third player, safety Jamarca Sanford, was a Christian. Childress couldn't get over the irony of the four men standing in the locker room, each making his own preparations to take the field in pursuit of a championship. For all their differences, they accepted one another and formed themselves into a close-knit team, dependent on one another to be successful. No one argued; no one came to blows; there was no division in the locker room. They would need to have one another's backs.

Childress reflected on the moment and began thinking about the Vikings' owner, Zygi Wilf, who is Jewish. It was September, and Wilf was preparing to celebrate the Jewish high holidays, which last ten days starting with Rosh Hashanah and culminating with Yom Kippur. During this period, God is supposed to decide who will live and die in the coming year, so it is a time of repentance and renewal.

"We start talking. And I'm telling them about the owner, and I'm trying to make some commonality with it," showing how although each worshiped differently, each of them cared deeply about their faith. "They are looking at me like I have ten heads. 'Why's Coach over here talking to me about this before the game?' But as a coach, it was a teaching moment," Childress says. "What you are trying to say to them—and what you hope they hear—is, 'Hey, just so you know, I recognize the fact that you are a Muslim. I never knew about Ramadan before. I just wondered why you were playing [crappy], why you look like you got no energy and are zapped. And you know what? You are because you couldn't eat when the sun is up.' [Abdullah] is not going to make accommodations, and I get that," Childress continues. "I respect him. I want to work with him because he's giving me 100 percent. Now, I'm always going to do what's best for the Minnesota Vikings. And they have to understand that. 'But we're a team, and I respect and love you.' I hope they heard that."

Mike Singletary shares Childress's point of view, which came as a surprise to many of his friends who had known him as a hard-nosed Christian during his playing days.

He says that when he first started coaching with the Baltimore

Ravens in 2003, his friends would call and say, "This is great. I know you are going to be witnessing to the guys."

But rather than lecture players who might not want to hear his message, Singletary wanted to set an example through the way he lived. "It's the biggest challenge we have as believers. I want my players to know there is something different about me. I don't have to talk about it. I don't have to pack my Bible around. But it's the way I deal with them. It's the way I am around them. It's the way I teach them. It's the way I discipline them. I want them to ask, 'Coach, what is it? What's different about you?' The greatest example I have is my life; it's my résumé. They ask, and then I can tell them my story."

Singletary says if he could go back in time, he'd lighten up a little. That's not to say he'd start boozing and womanizing, but maturity has taught him that by keeping his distance from what he perceived to be sinful activities, he was essentially ostracizing himself from the very people who could benefit from his friendship.

It's a fine line. And as a young man, it was probably easier to completely avoid the bars and the women in order to stay faithful. Now in his early fifties, Singletary's faith has grown, and his confidence and understanding of his own boundaries have developed too.

"The only thing I regret is that I was so black and white. I wouldn't go anywhere with anybody. 'I'm not going to the bar with you. I'm not going to the show with you. I'm not going to see this or that.' You know, there was a difference in me, but it was more pride than love.

"What I do now is I'll go out with a couple of coaches. If they order a beer, that's fine. I'll order a sparkling water. And let them talk about whatever subject they want. We can sit there and talk. But I want them to know that I love them and that I'll do anything for them. I'll meet them halfway, just so long as I don't cross the line where I'm overstepping my bounds with the Lord. The Holy Spirit will guide me with that."

Singletary says people ask him all the time, "How can you be in that locker room with those guys cursing all the time and being real tough?" He believes NFL players are some of the finest human beings you'd ever want to be around. He also knows that they are watching him. And they can't wait to call him a hypocrite. But the thing that's made him happiest since returning to the league as a coach is how often he meets up with former teammates and they ask him to pray with them, how often they say they wish they had found the church sooner, or how much they wish they had taken the time to talk to him about his faith back in the day.

The whole time, he says, they were watching.

"I've had a chance to kneel and pray with some of the toughest, most relentless guys the league has ever known. It just took time. And if I hadn't said no quite as often, perhaps Christ could have come into their lives sooner. Either way He's there now. And that's all that matters."

7

TRANSITIONS

One thing I do: Forgetting what is behind and straining toward what is ahead, I press on toward the goal to win the prize for which God has called me heavenward in Christ Jesus.

—Philippians 3:13–14

E very one of us eventually retires or gets fired, laid off, or bought out, either willingly or by a swift boot in the tail end. For some, it happens at the age of sixty or seventy and isn't all that unwelcome. For others, it hits at thirty or forty when there is a mortgage to pay, kids to feed, and aging parents to support.

Unemployment in the United States exceeded 9 percent when the 2011 football season began. Thousands more were being fired as industries restructured, economic growth sputtered, and debt-ridden countries around the world fought to stay solvent.

Men and women who had spent their whole lives in a particular profession weren't just getting fired; they were losing their personal identities. These were America's car guys, roofers, and bridge build-ers. Their skills were specific to an industry and while sure, they could retrain, who was hiring? And would it pay a living wage?

Savings were spent searching for a new job, and once those were gone, the bankers came. Based on data from CoreLogic Inc., between January 2010 and October 2011, 1.8 million homes went into foreclosure. With no buyers in the market, and banks skittish about lending, home values continued to plummet, eating away at home equity and leaving many borrowers underwater on their loans.

Mothers and fathers all over the US were losing their jobs, their savings, their homes, their identities, their respect, and their hope.

What is it they say about there being no atheists in foxholes?

For many, what helped them escape their shame and despair were the helping hand they received from their church, the love and support they felt from the congregation, and the belief in a brighter future that came from reading the Word.

Could they have saved more and spent less? Sure.

Should they have been taking classes and updating their skills to prepare for this day? Perhaps.

Should they have bought a smaller house, a less luxurious car, taken vacations closer to home? In hindsight . . . yes, yes, and yes.

What we have, we usually spend. And no matter how much we have, we are always foolishly rich in someone else's eyes.

Perhaps now, more than at any other time in recent memory, ordinary working people can relate to the experience of the NFL athlete and the emotional trials and tribulations he undergoes when he is thrown out of his job.

While a poor economy and inept political leadership have put America in a terrible state, similar upheaval and transition take place in the NFL every season as players are fired and then forced to relocate, retrain, and rebuild. Like the car guy at the General Motors plant who was laid off and fought to reestablish himself as a pool man, drywaller, or septic tank cleaner, so, too, the NFL player must pick himself up and start over.

Both sets of workers have been known to face bouts of depression and to fight with their wives over money, child rearing, and unemployment. Some turn to alcohol or an affair to dull the pain and rebuild their self-esteem, though that's hardly the solution to what troubles them. Others simply sit and sulk over their fate.

Players and chaplains who have been through the experience agree it's the men who maintain a good attitude and have faith in God and His plan for their lives, who usually get back to work the quickest and avoid the pitfalls that entrap a man struggling to rediscover himself and keep his family together during a difficult time.

MAKING YOUR WIFE MORE EFFICIENT

Ken Ruettgers was an offensive lineman at the University of Southern California, where he blocked for future NFL stars like Rodney Peete and Heisman Trophy winner Marcus Allen. He was selected by the Green Bay Packers in the first round of the 1985 draft and played for the Packers until his retirement following the 1996 season.

Ruettgers did a great job preparing for his second career. The former offensive tackle earned a business administration degree from USC, an MBA from California State University, and a PhD in sociology from Oxford Graduate School.

Today, he teaches sociology at Central Oregon Community College and runs a website, GamesOver.org, dedicated to helping former players get on with their lives.

The site is both sobering and encouraging, with sections on topics like "You Still Got What It Takes" and "Understanding the NFL Exclusive Rate: Cashing in Your Reality Check."

It also has articles addressing the hurdles players face, such as "The Top 10 Challenges of Transition":

1. Denial
2. Divorce
3. Financial Loss and Challenges
4. Physical Challenges
5. Lack of Significance and Purpose
6. Anger, Bitterness, and Jealousy
7. Loss or Change of Structure
8. Isolation
9. Substance Abuse
10. Depression

Ruettgers remembers what it was like after leaving the game that first year with no more workouts to attend, no schedule to follow, no game to prepare for, no teammates to meet up with. He was a young man of thirty-four, full of energy and vigor looking for a mission in life.

Then it happened. He was puttering around the house eating a snack when he stopped and took notice of the kitchen in a way he had never seen it before. *How is this room organized?* he asked himself. There was food, of course. And pots and pans and dishes and silverware. But were the items his family used most often the easiest to reach? And how were they placing items in the refrigerator? *Uh-huh, uh-huh,* he thought to himself. *This can be done better . . . I can improve this!*

"So I started driving my wife nuts, telling her how to be more efficient in the kitchen," he says, laughing. "I was going nuts. Two years later, I went to work for a publishing company, and it probably saved my marriage."

Like anyone changing careers, he had to make adjustments. But Ruettgers wasn't jumping from one job to another in the same industry. This was very different.

For the first time in his life, he was working five days on and two days off. NFL players get one day off during the season, and other than workouts and a few practices, they have the entire off-season to themselves.

"The intensity is different," Ruettgers admits. "In football you go hard for a period of time. But you can't work that pace year-round. You don't know that when you first get out of the league, so you go hard at everything, all the time, and then you are exhausted and you go home and you're thinking, *How do people do this?*

"And then you get to the weekend. Usually your day off is Tuesday. But now your weekend is everybody else's weekend, too, and there are the honey-dos and crowds at the park. And then come the paychecks. Wow! They look more like a per diem check than something to live on. And now you are in an entry-level job working for a per diem check five days a week, fifty weeks a year."

Ruettgers says Christians seem to do a better job finding coping mechanisms and suffer less with losing their celebrity status.

"If you are a Christian, the Bible calls us to be the lowliest," Ruettgers says. "Pro sports calls on us to be the highest. I think you will find that through the challenges these players faced, their transition from the NFL to their lives after the game is where their faith really grew. That's when they were stressed and life became difficult."

BELT-TIGHTENING

Danisha Rolle, wife of former NFL defensive back Samari Rolle, was asked what the hardest part of transitioning out of the NFL was for her family.

"When the game checks stopped," she answered directly. "You are making $30,000 to $40,000 a week, and then there is no income. So you have to adjust. It's like anyone else who loses a job or retires. No matter how much you have planned for the day, when it comes there is a reality, a sadness, to figuring out what you are going to cut back on and how you are going to do things differently."

Danisha and Samari are the sort of NFL couple others look up to. Samari played eleven seasons in the league and left with a nice nest egg. Danisha started a magazine called *SET*, and the couple even had the time to attend an abbreviated MBA program for retired athletes in the summer of 2011 at George Washington University in Washington, DC.

"You hear the stories of guys that have these financial advisers they trust, and it's not until they retire and get on top of their finances that they realize [they've] been duped or stolen from," Danisha says. "We're hearing about guys who thought they had $6 million or $7 million, and they don't because the money was invested badly. You feel, 'That will never happen to me,' but the reality is, it can."

Rolle is retired. He has money invested, and as long as he stays healthy, he can chart his future in a way most men will never know. It's the benefit of being one of the league's better players for more than a decade. Will they miss it? Sure, Danisha says. Game days were for family and friends and could be a great deal of fun. But in other ways, it was time to move on.

"It was a blessing to be able to say he had such a great career, but I believe that as you get older, your values change," she shares. "It was fun, the adrenaline of being able to have him playing in the NFL and getting dressed up and taking the kids to the game. But the guys are younger now; the women coming in are younger. You can mentor them, but you also feel like you are on to the next stage of your life. Each season in your life is about change, and you can embrace it or not. I welcome this stage of our lives. As one door closes, another opens, and we believe God will provide for us. What does the future hold? I'm sure He has a plan."

DETAILING THE FERRARI

Roman Oben planned for his post-NFL career, but it still wasn't easy. Born in Cameroon, West Africa, in 1972, Oben moved to Washington,

DC, nearly five years later when his mother took a position with the Cameroon embassy. After a stellar career at Louisville, where he earned a degree in economics, Oben was selected by the New York Giants in the third round of the 1996 draft. He played offensive tackle for the Giants, Cleveland Browns, Tampa Bay Buccaneers, and San Diego Chargers, retiring after the 2007 season. But he wasn't one of those players who rested on his laurels. Oben returned to school while he was playing for the Giants and earned a master's degree in public administration from Fairleigh Dickinson University. He also landed internships with Democratic congressmen Bill Pascrell of New Jersey and Dennis Kucinich of Ohio.

His first job after the pros was with the Corporate Playbook, an online job board that matched former college and pro athletes with companies that had sales openings. The company went under. He's now the northeast regional director for Advantage3, which finds sponsors for schools, hospitals, and other nonprofits. And he's a color analyst for MSG Varsity, a television channel dedicated to high school sports.

"I came out in 2008 when everyone lost their jobs and were hoping [President Barack] Obama would save the country," he says. "I had been preparing for that day all throughout my football career by doing congressional internships, corporate fellowships, and advancing my education. But the longer you play, the less time you are spending in the regular workforce developing your job skills, building relationships, and proving yourself.

"Your co-workers know in the first five minutes if you are smart or full of crap. There is a trust issue that has to be dealt with right away. Through your experience with them, they start to build up that trust. The first two months I was in the corporate world, they wondered, *Why is this guy in this building? He should be getting his Ferrari detailed. You are making less than $100,000 in a sales job* . . . so I showed up early and stayed late, read articles, and tried to grow my knowledge. You are that fifth grader trying to memorize the states again. Four, five, six months later, I started landing accounts. And then you start getting more support from those people who see you making that effort.

"People have to adjust to you, and you have to adjust to them. We go to T.G.I. Friday's for lunch. And we usually split it. And that is an adjustment too. Sometimes people are guarded. It's like they are saying, 'I know you made your money, but in my house, I'm the NFL player.' Sometimes as a man, you are forty-four years old, the head of your household, and some kid twenty-nine years old who played six years in the NFL pays for your lunch and that could be denigrating. 'I know you played in the NFL, but I can pay for my own lunch.'"

NOWHERE TO BE, NOTHING TO DO

Oben said one of the greatest challenges players face is a loss of structure, something that was mentioned in Ruettgers's "Top 10 Challenges of Transition" on GamesOver.org.

Athletes are told what time to lift weights, when to visit the trainer, when their position and team-wide meetings will be held, the day and time for Bible study, and they are often driven to promotional activities so they won't be late. Even their uniforms, pads, and shoes are cleaned and hung in their lockers for them.

Then they retire and are on their own.

"When you leave the NFL, you lose the structure . . . there is a time and place for things during your career. But when it's over, you have to create your own structure and be motivated. You have to make the calls and prepare for meetings without anyone blowing a whistle and telling you when to start or to stop or where to go. That's something people outside of football develop in their careers from an early age."

Change creates stress, anxiety, and loneliness, whether a man is playing football or counting cattle for a living. We all share the same emotions and fears.

Oben said it's even tougher on those who have been catered to from the time they were children through early adulthood. Having faith in God alleviates a lot of that stress because the individuals realize God has a plan for their lives and they see the bigger picture. It grants them a perspective that many nonbelievers struggle with.

"Faith helped me a lot because you are not consumed by the highs and lows," Oben says. "You are not consumed by your identity—the one that comes from your job or your salary. Whether you make $90,000 or $900,000, you are one of God's children.

"When you struggle to fit in, to start over, to create a new identity to the outside world and it all seems overwhelming, it's important to stop and remember that these are all opportunities to do something good. God wants to know what you are going to do with these opportunities or how you are going to overcome the negatives. God is asking, 'OK, I gave you a challenge here—what are you going to learn from this?'"

But even for the believers, it can be a difficult transition.

Oben used to have to protect his identity when he was traveling on vacation because people would perk up when they recognized him on the airplane and would want to talk the whole flight.

But once players retire and are no longer in the headlines, they quickly become has-beens. Fellow passengers whisper to their friends a little too loudly: "Hey, see that guy in the seat up there? Didn't he used to play football a long time ago? What's his name again? I can't remember . . ."

"When it ends, you discover your identity is now as a guy who *used* to play, and the guy who *used* to play isn't a great thing," Oben shares. "The difference in how people react to you is really noticeable.

"Look, not everyone is going to be a keynote speaker. Not everyone is a Super Bowl MVP. There are only so many Ray Lewises in life," says Oben, who won a Super Bowl championship with the Tampa Bay Buccaneers in January 2003. "Look at those guys who played four, five, six years on special teams. That guy returned home to the Midwest, and maybe he's coaching high school now. And in that small town, the people who hear he played football will ask, 'Do you miss it? What was the greatest part of playing in the NFL? Do you still talk to the guys?'

"You might as well carve your tombstone now because nothing you accomplish in your career is going to be greater than what you did playing football. Well, I don't believe that. The NFL is not a career; it's an opportunity. And it might last one year or five years.

"You don't know what life will bring. Once a guy leaves the league, 75 percent of them are trying to figure out who they want to be. And it's hard to start at the bottom in the Enterprise Rent-A-Car training program at thirty-two years old making $35,000 a year because you have real bills to pay. So when you want to discuss the difficulties of moving from the NFL to your second career, it's much deeper than most people want to go."

Oben will always remember something that former President Bill Clinton said at Coretta Scott King's funeral. Clinton said that she could have sat back and raised her children and been Dr. Martin Luther King's wife for the rest of her life and no one would have thought she was a failure. Instead, she fought for civil rights and kept his dream alive.

That really hit Oben, who decided that he, too, wanted to do something great with his life. He was determined not to sit back and say, "I played in the NFL. I don't need to do anything else."

He adds, "My faith was a tremendous part of helping make the transition out of football. You know, sometimes being a Christian, it doesn't mean someone in your family isn't going to get cancer or your parents won't get divorced or something negative won't happen.

"It just means that when it does happen, you have the foundation that you know that there is a lesson there, that you can learn from it, and that you will be a better, stronger person for going through that process. That is about having faith."

The difficulty players experience transitioning to a new career doesn't start the day they are fired. According to Oben, it starts when their parents, teachers, neighbors, and coaches turn them into stars years earlier.

"It's a problem when a fifteen- or sixteen-year-old kid is treated like an adult because he runs a 4.3 forty-yard dash and will get his family out of a bad financial situation," Oben says. "That kid will never have to grow up. He goes to the Southeastern Conference or the Big Ten and plays eight years in the NFL; and he has a line of people to support and now he is thirty-one, but inside, he's still that fifteen-year-old kid, only with bills and even more problems."

BORED WIVES, FAILING MARRIAGES

The NFL life can be glamorous for wives. Their husbands make a good deal of money, they live in beautiful homes, and they take lavish vacations. But when it's over, they suffer withdrawal and disappointment too. And if they haven't prepared for a post-NFL life by developing their own job skills, work contacts, and education, the afterlife can be a time for everything from depression and identity loss to divorce and abandonment.

"A lot of times, athletes don't encourage their wives to work, or the wives get content being stay-at-home wives or moms," says Octavia McDougle, wife of former NFL lineman Stockar McDougle. "Maybe it's that a lot of athletes look for that trophy wife that stays home and shops, but those relationships don't last long.

"When the player retires and there is nothing [for him] to do, and you are at home and you have nothing to do, and you are used to your own personal space because he hasn't been there the past five to ten years, you start to argue. You don't want someone coming in the house and telling you how to cook and clean and raise the kids. I've seen this happen over and over and over. You start bickering. They get under each other's skin and can't stand each other and now he's not working and he's starting to stress about finances and he's looking at you and you're wearing all these diamonds and you have all these handbags in the closet and he's like, 'You spent all my money.' And it's just a matter of time. Your days are numbered. You better get up to find a job. I've seen it, and it's disturbing. Hey, ladies, get yourself grounded in something. Go to school. Run his foundation. Start a business. Create a purpose in your life other than just staying home."

IT'S IMPORTANT TO GRIEVE

Corwin Anthony of Athletes in Action says for professional athletes, the shock of being cut and having to transition to the real world is certainly the most difficult challenge the athlete faces.

The NFL player's career didn't start after he graduated from college like it does for most of us. He's been playing football since Pop Warner. The pro game has been a goal for the player and his family from the time he was in the sixth or seventh grade. It's who he is, or at least, it's how he's perceived by almost all of his family and friends.

"It's a huge blow to who you are . . . your self-worth, your value," Anthony says. "A lot of athletes wrap up their value in the ability to perform, and when that's taken away, it's a huge hit to their identity."

Pastors try to head this off during players' careers by teaching them that even though they've had great success on the football field, they are not defined by what they do, but rather by who they are as a person.

"Your self-identity needs to be based on a much more stable, higher purpose away from playing this game. If football is all you are about, that is a pretty short-lived mentality," Anthony explains.

Chaplains remind players that God created them in His image "for a purpose that far exceeds their contribution on the football field," he continues. "They still have value; they can still make a difference and still have an impact on the next generation." Colossians 3:23–24 says: "Whatever you do, work at it with all your heart, as working for the Lord, not for human masters, since you know that you will receive an inheritance from the Lord as a reward. It is the Lord Christ you are serving."

Chaplains say football players and nonathletes alike are naturally going to feel a loss after being thrown out of their jobs. It's important to experience the sadness that comes with that loss.

"You have to grieve when this huge loss takes place in your life, and if you don't know how to grieve, then the whole transition can be painful and some guys don't recover from it," Anthony says.

"You have to have people in your life that know you and are not impressed by you, [family and friends] that you can process your pain with. All of us were taught that you toughen up. You stick it out. You try harder. And yet the Scriptures are full of principles that remind us how much we need each other to carry each other's burdens. If you don't have people in your life that can help you process your pain, you can depress it as long as you want, [but] it's going to bubble to the surface.

"Marriages fall apart," Anthony continues. "Guys are bankrupt, and part of it is because they are not processing the transition well. The key thing is having a community of people who can walk through that with you."

The emotional pain can be debilitating. And having a strong enough faith in God and a strong support system can help. But first, there is a practical side. And it's the one that smacks the player and his family in the face.

New York Giants chaplain George McGovern has counseled hundreds of athletes as they left the league, and he says the biggest question every player faces is: Who am I now?

According to McGovern, players have a hard time going from "it's all about me" to "it's not all about me." They were football players who were asked for autographs and had fans say how they wished they could swap lives with them for just one day. Then overnight the phone calls stop. The admiration stops. The celebrity functions stop. Restaurateurs, who used to find athletes a table, now let the athlete and his confused kids stand in line. "Those are emotional moments in an athlete's life," McGovern says.

Of course, the Joe Montanas and Emmitt Smiths and Dan Marinos of the world will always get a free pass. But the other 99 percent of former NFL players—the offensive lineman, the tight end, the defensive tackle who played for two or three or four years in the pros—are the ones who go from celebrity to "Who am I now?"

"A man's identity is not what he does, but who he knows he is on the inside," McGovern explains. "The guys who find their identity as a football player—or a mechanic or a salesman or a shipbuilder—are the guys who struggle most with the transition. But the man who knows he is a person who is loved by God, and who is in a relationship with God, and who would describe himself by saying: 'I am a child of God. I am created by God for a purpose and football is part of that purpose, but it's not the whole purpose. I'm a husband. I'm a father. I am a man who is on a mission to find God's purpose for my life.' Guys who think like that have a much smoother transition. I'm not saying it's a piece of cake, but it's a smoother transition than a guy whose identity is wrapped up in his performance on the football field."

McGovern says when players get cut, they often continue to train in hopes of getting called by another team. It might take a year or two before they give up the dream and accept that they need to start looking for a job in earnest. Meanwhile, they are burning through their savings as they continue to make mortgage payments on their big homes and perhaps another home for their mothers. Add hefty car payments to the mix, too, not to mention the money they loaned to their friends that they might as well forget about. Suddenly they are running out of cash, the bills are mounting, and they have no other career training to rely on.

He refers his players to a scripture from the Sermon on the Mount:

> *Do not store up for yourselves treasures on earth, where moths and vermin destroy, and where thieves break in and steal. But store up for yourselves treasures in heaven, where moths and vermin do not destroy, and where thieves do not break in and steal. For where your treasure is, there your heart will be also.* (Matthew 6:19–21)

"I try to be proactive by engaging guys in conversations when I get to a point where they trust me: 'You know, this thing isn't going to last forever. Have you thought about what you are going to be doing after football is over? Have you forced yourself to think about the transition out of football and into the next chapter of your life?'

"If you are not proactive, you are not doing the players a good service because you've got to force them to think about the possibilities and really the inevitability that this thing is going to be over sooner than they think."

McGovern continues, "I never had a guy deny that it's going to end. They acknowledge it intellectually, but heart-wise they've got so much invested emotionally and they are so passionate about making it that it's hard for their hearts to catch up to their minds and really embrace the inevitability of this transition."

Herb Lusk, the former Philadelphia Eagles running back and now the team's pastor, says it's about getting the right mind-set, whether you are a player or a factory worker.

"You are a replaceable commodity," he says. "You have to know that and not believe the lie, which is that you will be there forever and everyone loves you and you are wonderful.

"Even the coach who may be committed to you can't make any guarantees because the general manager or owner can come along and overrule him or trade you for a need the team has somewhere else. It's like a company. They cut entire divisions to save money, or they sell them off. Your boss can go too."

He says players have to identify what they want out of the game for themselves, for their families, and for the Lord. Is it to achieve great things on the football field? Is it to use the financial benefits to set themselves up for retirement? Is it to buy a home or to save money to put their children through school someday?

"When you are in football, there is no room for anything else. You eat, you sleep, you breathe the game. When somebody is cut or injured, you are eating and sleeping and breathing the game with someone else. The demands are so high. The machine keeps going. But when you are fired—now you are looking reality in the face, and you better know what's real."

Lusk says people are hurting in every neighborhood in America. It's relative. He recently talked to a member of his church who was laid off from a paper factory where he'd worked the majority of his life. The man was distraught, and Lusk knew there was nothing he could say to make the man feel better. Sometimes, he says, it's important to just be there to let them talk through their pain.

"What kind of answer are you going to give a person in that situation? I say that God is in control. And if you are one of God's children, according to the Scripture, God doesn't allow anything to happen to us without His permission. And ultimately we have to believe that God loves us enough that it will be some kind of move that will be good for us and our family in the long run. But yeah, it hurts. Doesn't matter what kind of a job you had. It hurts a lot."

ARE YOU PREPARING FOR THE INEVITABLE?

Troy Vincent played defensive back in the NFL for fifteen seasons, including eight with the Philadelphia Eagles. He was a five-time Pro Bowl player, who served as a player representative in the union and also started small businesses in health care, construction, and financial services.

He now works in the NFL's Office of Engagement, where he reaches out to current players about landing internships and finishing their college degrees, and to former players who need help writing résumés and finding employment.

He's in the ideal place to see players struggling to start a second career and find purpose in their lives. The voice mails he receives from these former players are often desperate pleas for help.

"In most cases, the player has never seen himself outside of the uniform, and it's sad. Our position is that if he engages with us in the process, we can help him. But it's not about what we can do for them; it's about what they can do for themselves."

The point Vincent was making is that no one is going to hand us lots of money or a great job or some huge opportunity when we're sitting on the couch. You can create all the programs you want for an employee, but if the worker doesn't have the initiative to walk into the manager's office and ask questions, then his failure rests solely on his own shoulders.

A few weeks after Vincent was born in 1970, an insurance salesman came to his grandmother's door and said he wanted to talk about the family's financial security. He eventually convinced her to buy a life insurance policy for her grandson. After paying $10,080 in premiums, the policy that man sold her was worth a grand total of $131. She had been taken, but wasn't financially savvy enough to know better.

Vincent's family never had a lot of money, so they didn't talk about it at the dinner table. The most popular investments in his Trenton, New Jersey, neighborhood were lottery tickets.

"We didn't know," Vincent said. "It's nothing we should be ashamed about. But we can do better now," he told *Bloomberg News.*

The league's engagement office provides career counseling and has a career transition program—for players one to five years removed from the game—that's offered four times a year.

Vincent says a lot of the calls he gets are from players who have been out of the league three or four years and are broke and running out of options. A typical conversation will go like this:

VINCENT: When was the last time you played?

PLAYER: Two thousand six, two thousand seven . . .

VINCENT: What have you been doing since then?

PLAYER: Really, nothing.

VINCENT: Have you graduated?

PLAYER: No.

VINCENT: OK, you've limited your options there. Have you connected back with your school?

PLAYER: No.

VINCENT: Have you connected back with your team?

PLAYER: No.

VINCENT: Have you reached out to any of your coaches?

PLAYER: No.

VINCENT: Can you send me your résumé?

PLAYER: What do you mean?

VINCENT: Résumés are a service we provide.

The NFL's engagement office reaches out to more than one thousand players each year, Vincent says. About three hundred to four hundred players leave the league annually and never return.

The engagement office gets a player's name once he hasn't been on an NFL roster a full year and he becomes eligible for severance pay.

The league has a three-day career transition program that offers services such as helping players identify their personality traits, providing speaking specialists, coaching one-on-one, making personal assessments of each player, and reviewing their NFL benefits.

"You have guys who have played six, seven, eight, nine years, and they don't have any idea where their benefits are. They didn't engage in the process," Vincent says. "As athletes, you don't pay attention. It's not a priority. You are just living in the moment. Everything is brought to you and given to you. It's a dream world, and those who transition well are those who remain grounded. We see that when the young men engage as student athletes at college, by going to the career counseling center, the student affairs office, when he has a relationship with the alumni association—he brings those traits to the NFL. So for him to get literature in his mail bin about a networking event, about resources, about online services, then it's not a foreign language to him."

Vincent says faith helps players deal with the difficult transition. "For me to say because of faith they do better, I can't say that. I can say the conversation we have is different. It's not desperation. He is much more receptive to constructive criticism. He's much more receptive and patient for the process moving forward; these are the things we need you to do, and we can meet you halfway. If that guy is not relying on faith, he is not looking beyond what he can see. Faith is not what you can see; faith is what you believe. The other guy is just saying, 'I can't eat tomorrow. I need to find some work.'

"There are more resources today than at any time in the history of the game. When athletes do not transition in and out well, [they have] made a conscious choice to do so," Vincent states.

Asked why they don't acknowledge they need help and seek it out, Vincent says, "Pride. Remember, when you don't stand on faith, what is the first thing that destroys you? Pride comes before the fall. That is the word of God. Pride is what keeps us from going to get help."

GOD'S PLAN

For God so loved the world that he gave his one and only Son, that
whoever believes in him shall not perish but have eternal life.

—John 3:16

There is a saying that "God is never late . . . but He is never early either." It means that God has a plan for our earthly lives, but that it will play out on His schedule and not on ours. Of course, this isn't much help. We'd prefer He deliver us a book in a three-ringed binder with a nice PowerPoint to walk us into the right career choices, investment opportunities, meaningful friendships, and idyllic love. How much easier it would be. But if we aren't allowed to fall down, we won't have to pick ourselves back up, gaining from the wisdom and confidence that come with a lesson well learned. These choices are a critical part of God's plan for us because they give us the freedom to make the most important choice of all: to follow Him.

Most of us struggle to hear God and to discern His wishes and direction in our lives, particularly when we are young. Sometimes we're sure we understand His plan, and when we are wrong, we become disappointed and wonder if there is any plan at all. We're too immature to see the push He gave us to choose one career over another, to pursue a crazy idea, or to love a person for reasons we can't fathom.

But as we age, we begin to connect the dots and oftentimes see that it was life's loneliest, most painful experiences that guided us out of the woods. Former Seattle Seahawks quarterback Matt Hasselbeck is somewhere in the midst of his journey, where he still struggles to fully understand God's plan. But despite his disappointment and uncertainty about some important moments in his life, his faith remains strong and resolute that the day is coming when it will be revealed to him.

> "For I know the plans I have for you," declares the Lord, "plans to prosper you and not to harm you, plans to give you hope and a future."
> (Jeremiah 29:11)

SEARCHING FOR MEANING

Moments before the Seattle Seahawks took the field for Super Bowl XL against the Pittsburgh Steelers at Ford Field in Detroit, Seahawks quarterback Matt Hasselbeck, backups Seneca Wallace and David Greene, and quarterbacks coach Jim Zorn gathered in the locker room for a pregame prayer.

Zorn, a devout Christian who had played quarterback for the Seahawks a generation earlier, was smiling "in a giddy sort of way," Hasselbeck remembers. They were all excited and bubbling with hope, and the conversation went like this:

ZORN: How awesome is this? We're in the Super Bowl. How awesome is this?
HASSELBECK: It's awesome.
ZORN: How cool is God? The story of the year is so cool.

HASSELBECK: Yeah, it's really cool. This is the Super Bowl. It's a dream come true.

ZORN: But you know what also is cool? It's that whether we win or lose this game, He's still God. He's still in control. And He's still got a plan that's going to be amazing no matter what.

HASSELBECK: Yeah, yeah, yeah. No doubt, man, we'll thank Him win or lose.

The Seahawks were one of the National Football League's best stories during the 2005 season. After starting 2-2, they reeled off eleven straight victories before losing the season finale to Green Bay to finish 13-3. They had the NFL's top offense, scoring 452 points. Running back Shaun Alexander, who led the league in rushing with 1,880 yards and scored a record 28 touchdowns, was named the league's Most Valuable Player. And Hasselbeck had a Pro Bowl year, completing 65.5 percent of his passes for 3,459 yards, with 24 touchdowns and only 9 interceptions. Play-off victories over the Washington Redskins (20–10) and Carolina Panthers (34–14) sent Seattle to its first Super Bowl in the franchise's thirty-year history.

The season came together so miraculously that the faithful had begun to believe it couldn't be mere coincidence and that the heavenly Father must have had a hand in it. Hasselbeck, who would be voted to three Pro Bowls during his ten-year stint in Seattle, was one of them. Two weeks before the Super Bowl, team chaplain and close friend Karl Payne approached Hasselbeck in the locker room. "He said, 'Listen, this is a verse I need to share with you. I think it's important. It really applies to your life.'" The verse was 1 Peter 5:6: "Humble yourselves, therefore, under God's mighty hand, that he may lift you up in due time."

Hasselbeck understood what the chaplain was getting at. He'd gone through so much in his life to reach pro football's grandest moment, and the verse reminded Hasselbeck, "It's not on my time; it's on His time." Hasselbeck reflects back to that day. "And I'm thinking, *I'm humbling myself here in all these interviews before the Super Bowl. I'm using them as an opportunity to talk about the influence God had on our team and how many faithful guys we have.* And I'm thinking to God, *All this, it's not about me; it's about You. It's not about me; it's about everybody else.* And I'm feeling this is amazing, and I can see how all this is playing out. This is my time. This is part of His plan for me. We're going to win this. We're going to do it."

RAIN, SNOW, AND HARD TIMES

Hasselbeck was born in Boulder, Colorado, where his father, Don, had met Matt's mother, Mary Beth "Betsy," when Don was an All-American tight end at the University of Colorado. He was drafted by the New England Patriots in 1977 and had stints with the Oakland Raiders, Minnesota Vikings, and New York Giants over a nine-year NFL career that exposed his three sons to some of the greatest players of all time.

Don and Betsy developed a close bond with the Lord when the kids were still in elementary school, and Christianity had a strong influence on Matt and his little brothers, Tim, who also played quarterback in the NFL, and Nathanael, who was a wide receiver at the University of Massachusetts.

Matt says God's plan for his life as an NFL quarterback was rooted in his high school and college years, though he couldn't possibly know it at the time.

"My senior year, it rained, sleeted, or snowed every game. It was unbelievable. I mean, it was unfair. I remember praying to God, 'What is going on? What is Your problem here? Help a brother out,'" he says with a laugh. He adapted to throwing a cold, wet ball and led Xaverian Brothers High School in Westwood, Massachusetts, to the

Division 1-A Super Bowl where his team led 17–0 entering the fourth quarter, only to lose 18–17.

A few months later, he started school at Boston College, where he would meet his future wife, Sarah, during freshman orientation. After four years at an all-boys Catholic school, Hasselbeck admits that his main goal that day was to sit next to the most beautiful girl in class. When they started selecting their courses, Hasselbeck looked over Sarah's shoulder and copied her schedule verbatim. He received kudos from his adviser for taking such an ambitious course load of accounting, calculus, history, geology, and philosophy.

"I just went for it," says Hasselbeck, now the father of two girls and a boy.

Hasselbeck graduated with a degree in finance and marketing. Sarah, an All-American field hockey player and now member of the Boston College Varsity Club Athletic Hall of Fame, studied accounting and graduated summa cum laude.

They married in June 2000, and looking back on it, he thinks meeting Sarah was probably the highlight of his experience at Boston College.

He had a different coach just about every year, fell to the bottom of the depth chart after a blowup with Coach Dan Henning, and led the team to a not-so-stellar 8-13 record as a starter.

"All throughout that period, I was really struggling," Hasselbeck admits. I'm like, 'Why can't I have consistency and continuity?' I really got into the tank with a new coaching staff, and I viewed myself as a second- or third-string quarterback. They didn't play me, and I had no answers and was praying to God, but was also feeling like, 'What's the deal here?'

"I got a letter from my dad. He knew I was hurting. He had been through it as a player—cut and traded and hurt and benched and started—and he sent me a letter that said, 'Hang in there, Proverbs 3:5–6.'" ["Trust in the LORD with all your heart and lean not on your own understanding; in all your ways submit to him, and he will make your paths straight."]

"I had no idea what verse that was. He wrote it out, and it was like, 'All right, I have no idea why this is happening, but I will trust You, God.' The next week the coaches put in a fake field goal for me to run against Notre Dame, our biggest game, and it wasn't a throw. It's not even a quarterback play; it's a field goal holder play, but it was a huge play. It was fourth-and-eight, and I got the eight yards and inside. It felt like He was saying, 'Hey, I'm with you.' It was a difficult time."

Though the changing coaching staffs were hard to adjust to, Hasselbeck was working with some of the best quarterback coaches in the game, something he would come to understand and appreciate later in his life when things really got tough.

BUILDING REFERENCES, GAINING WISDOM

His head coaches at BC included Tom Coughlin, Dan Henning, and Tom O'Brien. His offensive coordinators were Dirk Koetter, Steve Kragthorpe, and Jeff Jagodzinski. And he had four quarterback coaches in Gary Crowton, Koetter, Kragthorpe, and Don Treadwell.

"When it came time to be drafted, Andy Reid was the quarterback coach at Green Bay and he was friends with two guys who were my quarterback coaches [at Boston College] and they said nice things about me—the type of person I was, the character I had, and Andy saw a glimmer of potential in me."

Hasselbeck was selected by Green Bay in the sixth round of the 1998 draft. He was the seventh quarterback chosen that year after Peyton Manning, Ryan Leaf, Charlie Batch, Jonathan Quinn, Brian Griese, and John Dutton.

He was waived by the Packers and then re-signed to the team's practice squad. Green Bay was coming off consecutive Super Bowl appearances—a victory over the New England Patriots and a loss to the Denver Broncos—and was led by perennial Pro Bowl quarterback Brett Favre.

Hasselbeck sat the bench for three seasons learning from one of the greatest quarterbacks of his generation before he was traded to Seattle in 2001.

"I get drafted by the Green Bay Packers with a great team and great staff, but the weather is cold. Then I go play in Seattle, and it's raining all the time. Guys who are first-round picks are freaking out and panicking about the cold and the rain. Well, guess what? I've played in snow. I've played in sleet. I've played in rain, and I know how to handle it because I experienced it all the time in high school and actually quite a bit in college. No big deal."

Between the time Hasselbeck was drafted by the Packers in 1998 and the time he was named the Seahawks' starter the final time in 2002, he'd changed head coaches four times (Mike Holmgren, Ray Rhodes, Mike Sherman, and Mike Holmgren again), offensive coordinators three times (Sherman Lewis, Tom Rossley, and Gil Haskell), and quarterback coaches four times (Andy Reid, Mike McCarthy, Tom Rossley, and Jim Zorn). Sounds a lot like his college experience, doesn't it?

"I've had a lot of coaching turnover, so I'm getting used to having all these different coaches," Hasselbeck says.

"I look back at all those hard times, and I'm like, 'I would have done it differently. I would have made it easier for myself—smooth sailing.' But the trials I went through prepared me for my career."

Hasselbeck, who signed a three-year contract with the Tennessee Titans in 2011, says his favorite scripture, the one he often adds to autographs, is Colossians 3:23:"Whatever you do, work at it with all your heart, as working for the Lord, not for human masters."

The passage concludes in verse 24:"since you know that you will receive an inheritance from the Lord as a reward. It is the Lord Christ you are serving."

"You don't always love your coach. You don't always feel up to practicing. Sometimes you are injured. But you go out and give it all you've got anyway because you feel as if you are doing it for the Lord," Hasselbeck says. "If someone was ever asking about me and they said, 'What's that guy all about?' I'd hope this is what people would say about me; that I always gave it all I had, and I did it for the Lord."

KEEPING THE FAITH

The Pittsburgh Steelers were four-point favorites to win Super Bowl XL in February 2006, but the Seahawks came out fighting and made it a contest to the very end.

Seattle trailed 14–10 with 10:54 left in the fourth quarter and was driving down the field. On third-and-18 from the Pittsburgh 27-yard line, Hasselbeck lofted a pass over the head of receiver Darrell Jackson that was intercepted by Steelers cornerback Ike Taylor at the 5-yard line.

Four plays later, the Steelers ran a gadget play and iced the game.

On first-and-10 from the Seattle 43-yard line, Ben Roethlisberger pitched the ball to Willie Parker running left, who handed off to receiver Antwaan Randle El coming back right on the reverse.

While the defense ran one way and then the other, receiver Hines Ward—the game's Most Valuable Player—slipped downfield unnoticed. El, a quarterback at Indiana, passed deep to Ward, who caught the ball for a touchdown with 9:04 left in the game to put Pittsburgh ahead by the final score of 21–10.

Despite playing poorly—converting only 9 of 21 passes for 123 yards, with no touchdowns and two interceptions—Roethlisberger became the youngest quarterback ever to win a Super Bowl. Meanwhile, Hasselbeck completed 26 of 49 passes for 273 yards, one touchdown, and one interception in the loss.

Steelers running back Jerome Bettis, a six-time Pro Bowl player who grew up in the Motor City, retired after winning his first Super Bowl championship.

And Steelers coach Bill Cowher, who had coached the team to nine postseason appearances in the previous thirteen seasons, finally had his Super Bowl title.

The loss was heartbreaking for Hasselbeck and his teammates, some of whom thought they were destined to go home Super Bowl champions.

Hasselbeck had suffered many disappointments in his life—having the loss in the high school championship game, sitting the bench in college, getting cut from the Packers and re-signed to the practice squad, losing his starting job for a time in Seattle—but this was the toughest.

"I really felt like I was ready for that game and that our team was ready for that game, and we didn't play our best. It's hard. That sticks with me," he shares. "Who knows why that happened? I guess I can know confidently that God is in control. He has a plan. And I just have to be humble, faithful, and trust that His plan is way better than my plan."

As the game came to a close, confetti rained from the sky. Steelers players jumped and hugged one another, rejoicing in their victory. Team executives, coaches, and key players moved onto a temporary stage for the presentation of the Vince Lombardi Trophy. And in the background, through the confetti and black and gold jerseys, a small cadre of Seahawks players could be seen gathering around the 50-yard line and taking a knee. Their faces were emotionless as they watched the celebration happening around them. They were clearly stunned, and yet they seemed to be waiting.

"We were allowing them to have their time," Hasselbeck recalls. "They earned it. They deserved it. But it's hard. We'd given it everything we had. I thought I understood how it was going to play out. I was so sure. I felt for sure it was our time.

"We watched them. We were sitting there waiting to say the [postgame] prayer and they were taking pictures of us and it was like, 'OK, this is the last thing I feel like doing right now. But I'm going to be obedient. And I'm going to trust.' So we prayed to the heavenly Father and gave thanks."

SEEING THE FOREST FOR THE TREES

No one gets fired and thinks, *Great, this will probably lead to a better job.*

Who among us has been dumped by a girlfriend and thought, *Fabulous, I'll probably meet the love of my life now that my girlfriend has ripped my heart out and left me for another guy?*

Is there anyone who gets reassigned to manage the worst division in the company and says to himself: "What an opportunity. Twenty years from now this division will be the most profitable in the company. I'll be in line for CEO!"?

Former Indianapolis Colts coach and current NBC analyst Tony Dungy says he always told his players to practice hard, believe in their fellow teammates, and have faith in God's plan for them. But even as he was speaking the words, he knew what he was asking was a tall order, especially for young men who don't have enough life experience to believe in what can't be seen or touched.

He knows because he lived through it himself and now offers his own life experience in hopes that others will understand God's plan for them in ways they didn't before.

Dungy grew up in Jackson, Michigan, where he was a standout quarterback for Parkside High School before moving on to play at the University of Minnesota. He was featured in *Sports Illustrated*'s "Faces in the Crowd" column in the January 26, 1970, edition, which profiled the athletic accomplishments of the fourteen-year-old prep star. His life was one success after another, and he naturally assumed he would enjoy a long career in the NFL. That's why it was such a shock when no one drafted him.

"It was a major crisis in my life," Dungy shares. "Nobody wanted me, and I couldn't figure out why. It was the first time in my life that I wasn't successful at something I really wanted to do."

The upside to not being selected in the NFL draft is that you can shop yourself around. Dungy landed a tryout with Coach Chuck Noll's Pittsburgh Steelers in 1977, but they insisted he change positions and move to defensive back. What? Everything would be new. It would be like starting over. After he thought it over, Dungy realized that he didn't have any options. He was beside himself with emotion. "I really thought that was the end of the world for me. First, no one wanted me, and then when I found a team, they didn't want me to do what I was best at."

Dungy made the most of his opportunity. He played two seasons in Pittsburgh, leading the team in interceptions (6) his second year, and helped the team win Super Bowl XIII with a 35–31 victory over the Dallas Cowboys. Before the champagne had time to warm up, the Steelers traded their up-and-coming defensive back to the San Francisco 49ers, where an upstart named Bill Walsh was trying to build the worst team in the NFL into a contender.

"Why me?" wondered Dungy. "Why, why is this happening to me? Isn't this a shame? How many times can these terrible things happen?"

Dungy injured his knee in his first and only season with the 49ers, bringing an end to a once-promising career. The story didn't end there, of course. But as Dungy notes, there is no way of knowing that when you are twenty-four years old and your whole world comes crashing down on your head.

Looking back on it now, he says, it's easy to see the plan God had drafted for the aspiring quarterback who once graced the pages of *Sports Illustrated* and had such great plans for a pro football career.

"God was preparing me to be a coach," Dungy says. "Think about it. He took me from being a quarterback, an offensive player, and then made me a defensive player. I played for a championship team in Pittsburgh in the midst of a run of four Super Bowls and watched how Coach Noll ran that team and kept us sharp. Then I went to a rebuilding team and saw how Bill Walsh put it together. But going through it, not knowing what was happening, unable to see His plan, it was just a series of 'Why, why, why, why?' So you learn over time that things that look like negatives or pitfalls aren't. God does have a plan. All you can do is to keep working hard to get through the challenges and obstacles and tests and have faith."

Dungy's special teams coach on that awful San Francisco team was a bright young coach named Dennis Green, and the two hit it off. Years later, Green, then the coach of the Minnesota Vikings, hired Dungy as his defensive coordinator, where Dungy made a name for himself and started getting head coaching interviews.

If it seems that the moral lesson is over, hold on.

Dungy, finally out of his youth and now certain of God's plan for him to pursue coaching, hit another series of disappointments and rejections. It was something that Dungy never quite got used to, but eventually learned to accept.

"I'd go into these job interviews and explain my plan for turning around the franchise and the owners would nod patiently and ask a question and then when I finished, they would say, 'I just don't think that will work. It sounds great, and it might have worked as a defensive coordinator, but I don't see how that will ever work as a head coach.' And out the door I'd go.

"You start second-guessing yourself. Even at that point in my career and my life and my faith, I was still affected by all this, and I'd think, *The next time I get an interview, should I change what I'm saying or just keep my mouth shut altogether and play 'the game' in order to get the job?*

"I thought about that a long time. I struggled with it," he says. "And then I came to the conclusion that I've got to be myself. And if that's not what they are looking for, then it's not what was meant to be. I say it with a lot more confidence in my voice now than I did then. But I decided I had to stay true to myself, my family, and my faith. And eventually, it all worked out."

THE DAY FOOTBALL FOUND ITS FAITH

He said to them, "Go into all the world and preach the gospel to all creation. Whoever believes and is baptized will be saved, but whoever does not believe will be condemned." (Mark 16:15–16)

Historic moments sometimes announce themselves with gunshots or sirens or the crush of bodies pushing against one another. Other times, the moment comes and goes with hardly a notice and takes many years to reveal itself as something with the power to change our culture. That's how it was for Herb Lusk the morning of October 9, 1977, when a simple moment of worship changed the sports world forever.

Lusk's Philadelphia Eagles were playing the New York Giants in the Meadowlands that day. It was the fourth quarter, and Coach Dick Vermeil sent in the play: 48 Toss. Quarterback Ron Jaworski, now an analyst for ESPN, took the snap and pitched the ball to Lusk, who ran around left end. The Eagles' halfback sped outside, broke into the Giants' secondary, and raced 70 yards for a touchdown.[1]

As a crowd of 48,824 looked on, Lusk took a few steps into the end zone and did something no professional athlete had ever done before. He dropped to his left knee, bowed his head in prayer, and thanked God. It was a game-changing moment in American sports. Every baseball player who's ever pointed to the sky, every soccer player who crossed himself, every football player who has ever taken

---

1. http://www.washingtonpost.com/wp-dyn/content/article/2007/09/27/ AR2007092702077.html/?hpid=sec-religion.

a knee—all of them came *after* Herb Lusk. It was the first time a player expressed his faith as part of a touchdown celebration, and it opened the door for thousands of others to follow.

"I just said, 'Thank You, Jesus,'" Lusk remembers. "It was personal, and nobody made a big deal out of it at the time. It wasn't until later that I realized it was significant. Hey, somebody's got to be the first guy. And now, I think that might have been God's purpose for me playing in the NFL all along."

It didn't seem that way on October 9. It was Lusk's second touchdown of the day and sealed the Eagles' 28–10 victory. None of the newspapers covering the game mentioned his prayer, choosing instead to focus on his 117 rushing yards. The Eagles' players knew Lusk to be a faithful person and thought it was in character that he might take a moment to pray and didn't make anything out of it. The only person who said anything was Carl Peterson, the Eagles' director of player personnel, who warned him that his praying could earn the team a delay-of-game penalty.

Although Lusk was later credited for this groundbreaking moment, it wasn't actually the first time he'd knelt down in prayer after scoring a touchdown. Lusk tore ligaments in his right knee his junior year at Long Beach State and was told he'd never play again. After a long and painful rehabilitation, Lusk proved the doctors wrong. He earned his starting job back and rushed for 1,596 yards and scored 16 touchdowns in 1975. He was the nation's second-leading rusher that season, averaging 145.1 yards per game, and was eighth in all-purpose yards, averaging 150.7 yards. Lusk was so grateful for his recovery that he began thanking God every time he scored, earning him the nickname "The Praying Tailback."

"I prayed a lot during my road to recovery, asking God for another chance," Lusk recalls. "He gave it to me, and I started thinking about how I could say thank you. Christians have to be public in their faith; it is part of growing the church. So I thought, *How can I show the world that I have a relationship with Jesus Christ that is personal and real?* The only thing I had was football. So I said, 'I'll make the end zone my pulpit. I'll get in there as many times as I can, and every time I get in there, I'll kneel down and pray.'"

Lusk's love for God came honest. His father was a Baptist preacher who required his son to attend church and worship daily. His parents struggled in their relationship, though, and split. His father moved from their home in Memphis, Tennessee, to Monterey, California, to start over. But Herb would soon be reunited with his father. Lusk was fifteen when Martin Luther King Jr. was assassinated on the balcony of the Lorraine Motel in Memphis, Tennessee, on April 4, 1968. His mother was afraid her rambunctious son would eventually get caught up in the riots, so she sent him to live with his father in California. Herb would accept Jesus Christ as his Savior a year later and begin leaning toward a future in the ministry.

He made that clear when he was selected by the Eagles in the tenth round of the 1976 National Football League draft. He told reporters that he was going to play three seasons and then quit and join the ministry. Everyone laughed, of course. No one quits the NFL. A player has to be thrown out. Lusk returned to the Eagles' training camp at Widener University for the start of training camp in 1979—his fourth season. After the first day of camp, he awoke to a strange feeling, prayed for guidance, and knew that was it. He walked away that morning and started a ministry.

"I played three years and quit on my own," says Lusk, who rushed for 483 yards and two touchdowns in three NFL seasons. He earned $65,000 his best year. "I wasn't the greatest running back in the league. Looking back on it, it's very clear to me that the prayer in the end zone was my role," Lusk says. The only rushing touchdowns of his career came on that day. But more than three decades later, he is still remembered for kneeling in the end zone. "It opened a lot of opportunities for me to share my faith and why I do what I do and why I believe what I believe. I spoke at college campuses, and I spoke all over the country."

Lusk is the Eagles' team chaplain today, though he's probably made a greater impact on society as the pastor at Greater Exodus Baptist Church in Philadelphia and as founder of People for People, Inc., a not-for-profit arm of the church, whose mission is to help the poor. When Lusk became pastor in 1982, the church had seventeen members. Today, it counts more than fifteen hundred active members and holds three services on Sundays. People for People operates out of an adjacent eight-story building that houses a charter school, daycare center, and youth mentoring center. It also offers job training to welfare recipients and helps former prison inmates get training and jobs. Lusk's hard work hasn't gone unnoticed. He spoke from the pulpit of the Greater Exodus Baptist Church via satellite feed during the 2000 Republican National Convention and served as an adviser to President George W. Bush, who twice visited Greater Exodus, gave People for People financial report as part of his administration's faith-based initiatives, and had Lusk sleep over at the White House on three occasions.

TRUSTING IN GOD

If there was ever a Christian who deserved for good things to happen to him, it was Mark Brunell.

The former Jacksonville Jaguars quarterback started a church out of his living room in Jacksonville, Florida, that has grown to more than two thousand members. He tithes, even when the checks are for six-figure amounts. He's been a devout believer since he gave his life to Christ as a college sophomore. And he has used his wealth for good, starting a foundation that has raised nearly $1 million to help critically ill children and their families.

But despite all the hard work he's put in on the playing field and all the good he's done for his community, Brunell keeps coming up short of the goals he has worked so hard to achieve.

He was selected in the fifth round of the 1993 NFL draft by the Green Bay Packers as a backup to Brett Favre. Two years later, he was traded to the expansion Jacksonville Jaguars, where he became an icon overnight.

Brunell, who holds Jaguars franchise records for most passing yards in a season (4,367), most passing yards in a career (25,698), and most pass completions in a season (353), led Jacksonville to AFC Conference championships in 1996 and 1999, only to lose both games just one win shy of the Super Bowl.

When he finally made it to the league championship, it was in February 2010 and he was a backup to Drew Brees, the New Orleans Saints' Super Bowl MVP who led his team to a 31–17 victory over the Indianapolis Colts.

Even though Brunell was one of the NFL's most successful quarterbacks in his era, he never quite got the golden ring the way he had hoped. And he experienced similar struggles in his private life off the field.

After earning more than $50 million in his first fifteen NFL seasons, Brunell filed for bankruptcy in June 2010 with $5.5 million in assets and $24.7 million in liabilities because of failed real estate and development investments he had made just before the housing bubble popped and the country fell into a deep recession.[2]

So what is the point to living a godly life, raising your family under the tenets of the church, sharing your worldly fortune with others, and spreading your religion through word of mouth and deed if there is no benefit to it? Aren't you supposed to be rewarded if you follow the rules and live the life Christ expects of you?

---

2. http://jacksonville.com/sports/football/jaguars/2010-06-29/story/
bankrupt-former-jaguars-quarterback-mark-brunell-owes-247.

"I think the day we give our lives to Jesus, that is the payoff," Brunell says during an interview at his home in the summer of 2011. "There is no promise of an easy life. In the Bible, Jesus says *when* the storms come, not *if* the storms come, but *when*. When you become a Christian, you aren't guaranteed a problem-free existence. Life throws things your way. But I know one thing: the payoff ultimately is that you spend eternity with the Father. Everybody knows that regardless of how difficult this life is, that's the ultimate payoff."

Most people would probably be forgiven if they were angry or bitter after finishing one step short of their lifelong goal or if they had just been publicly dragged through bankruptcy with reporters detailing their every asset and liability. But Brunell seems unfazed, choosing to view the good he did for the city of Jacksonville and various charities as successes. Ultimately his travails are part of God's bigger plan for his life—one, admittedly, he can't figure out just yet.

Even though he has fallen short of his goals, the ride has been pretty spectacular. Brunell grew up in Santa Maria, California. His father was his high school coach and athletic director, and his mother worked for a title insurance company. Brunell made the varsity baseball team as a freshman and the varsity football team as a sophomore. While his athletic talents made him a leader on the sports field, his youth and immaturity made him a follower off it, he says. And though he attended a few Bible school camps and church youth groups that he thought were fun, he didn't make a commitment to the Lord until much later.

"Whatever the cool kids were doing, I wanted to do. I just wanted to fit in and to find my place," he says. "There is a big difference between a freshman and a senior in high school, and I was exposed to things I shouldn't have been—basically, drinking. So while I was active in my youth group, I was still very active socially and trying to find my place."

Brunell earned a scholarship to the University of Washington in

Seattle where he discovered his freedom: "I made my own rules and jumped into everything college had to offer." Brunell was leading a double life, and it gnawed at him. He said he knew full well that he was off course, but he was driven to see what was out there. "I knew the difference between right and wrong, and I knew that if I continued on that path it wouldn't be a good thing."

Brunell was invited to a campus outreach his sophomore year and went because he didn't have anything better to do. It had been quite a while since he'd gone to church or a Bible study. *Why not?* he thought. Then it happened, in the same way it's happened to generations of Christians. He started listening to the speaker share the gospel and snap! "It was as if that speaker was speaking right to me," Brunell says. "I remember the conviction I felt that night. I remember thinking, *I'm way off. I know better.* I was doing OK in football, and I wasn't doing poorly in school, but inside I was just off track and needed to decide whether I was going to be a Christian and live the life God wanted me to live or just be like everyone else."

This was a tough call for Brunell. Imagine him at nineteen, attending a Division 1 school on a football scholarship. Women were easy to come by, drinks were on the house, school was going OK, and unlike his high school years, he oozed "cool" from every pore in his body.

Alone in his thoughts, Brunell would battle the wild boy inside him and couldn't decide what he wanted more—to party and have fun or to live a righteous life. If God is forgiving and a granter of second chances, wouldn't it be OK if he committed to Christ *after* he had his fill of the good times?

No.

Mark was reaching that age in life where he couldn't lie to himself anymore. He understood the choice he faced and the consequences of that choice.

"Whether I had the courage to live as a Christian completely was the issue," he explains. "Could I keep living in church one way and in the locker room the other? The question for me was, 'Who am I going to be?'"

When Brunell was in high school, he was sort of alone with his religious beliefs, he says. He had Christian friends at church. But there was really no one at school to walk with or hold him accountable or go to Bible study with when he felt alone.

But when he turned to his faith in college, he had a teammate in Todd Bridge, whom he could lean on when he needed support. It made all the difference and enabled Brunell to make the commitment in college that he just wasn't mature enough to make in high school. Brunell and Bridge both began walking with Christ during Brunell's sophomore year at Washington, and they are still friends to this day. "I had someone there to walk with, and that was a huge difference because I wasn't alone," Brunell says. "It wasn't even that hard. I was so convicted and so excited because it was the first time that it felt like a real commitment. It was like walking into that outreach on campus; I knew they were genuine, authentic . . . I felt like, 'Gosh, these people are the real deal. Whatever these guys have, I want it.'"

Brunell says he embraced Christianity so fully that getting rid of the music and stopping drinking and chasing women were a piece of cake. In hindsight, that was the easy part, he admits now. "As I started living this way, it was such a complete turnaround, it started getting tough with my teammates because they knew something was different. But I had a buddy there, which made it easier. I made the decision that I was going to make the Lord the number one thing in my life. I was going to make Him Lord over everything: school, football, my relationships, the way I talked, the way I acted, the way I thought. So that was a real big difference for me, and it was a pretty cool moment."

Brunell became a starter for Washington his sophomore season in 1990 and led the team to the Pac-10 championship. He was named the Most Valuable Player in the Rose Bowl that year after guiding the Huskies to a 46–34 victory over Big Ten champion Iowa. Washington finished the season ranked number five and had great promise for the following year.

But Brunell injured his knee in the spring game and only played sparingly his junior season, usually entering games well after they had been decided. In that year's Rose Bowl, he shared time with Billy Joe Hobert to pass for 281 yards and three touchdowns to lead Washington past Michigan, 34–14.

Mark had met his wife, Stacy, a Huskies cross-country runner, in the weight room during his second year of college. She invited him to a sorority event, and then they went roller-skating. The couple married, and three months before his senior season, they had the first of their four children, a daughter named Caitlin, who is now attending the University of Alabama.

For Brunell's senior year, he shared the quarterback position with Billy Joe Hobert, then moved into the starting spot the final three games. He led the Huskies to a share of the Pac-10 title and a third straight Rose Bowl, a 38–31 loss to Michigan.

Brunell says he was riding high that winter. He was growing in his religious life, was married to a beautiful bride, and had an adoring daughter. While injury cut short what could have been an outstanding college career, he was happy and had proven himself deserving of a shot in the National Football League.

He was selected by the Green Bay Packers in the fifth round of the 1993 draft to back up Brett Favre, but was traded to the expansion Jacksonville Jaguars two years later for a third- and fifth-round draft pick.

Brunell made friends quickly in his new hometown, and a year after joining the club, he started a Bible study with a few teammates and some friends in his living room.

"It was real relaxed," Brunell says. "We'd have dinner or something and then the study afterwards. That first night we ever had it, there were probably five or six of us, and four guys gave their lives to the Lord that night. [Pro Bowl offensive lineman Tony] Boselli got baptized in the pool. There were quite a few guys who got baptized in the pool. My pool was pretty popular. It was a real intimate group. We'd hang out, and you think it's going to last forever."

Players started bringing their wives and girlfriends until about 20 percent of the team was attending the meetings. In time, Brunell's little Bible study outgrew his house, so they started holding meetings in a nearby Marriott ballroom. And when it grew too big for the Marriott, they put together funding and started Southpoint Community Church.

This church and the relationships he's forged in his community are every bit as important, if not more so, than the Super Bowl ring, the AFC championship games, and the three Pro Bowls. Brunell is sure of this, and yet he still doesn't know what God's plan is for his life. "I would have loved to get a Super Bowl [in Jacksonville], but it didn't happen," he says. "I'm disappointed, and honestly I think about it often. But maybe I wasn't supposed to for whatever reason. I don't think it is punishment or anything like that; it's just God's plan for me.

"I think the Christian life is boiled down to two things: you obey and you trust. You obey God and trust that whatever happens, hey, it's His plan for your life."

As for the bankruptcy, "I believe that it's God's plan that something in my life needs to be developed. I know as far as money was concerned, I needed to learn a lot. I know it has developed character in me. I'm learning about people. I'm learning about finance and business, and perhaps there is a measure of discipline in there too."

His favorite scripture is Jeremiah 29:11: "'For I know the plans I have for you,' declares the LORD, 'plans to prosper you and not to harm you, plans to give you hope and a future.'"

Brunell says the one thing he is sure of is that when you put Jesus before every decision, every thought, and every action, things will be OK. "I know that God has a plan for me. I know that regardless of any struggles I go through, it's for a reason," he says.

Sitting in a living room chair, dressed in a T-shirt, shorts, and flip-flops on a warm June afternoon, Brunell throws a watchful eye to his two sons who are being home-schooled, and recites Romans 8:28: "And we know that in all things God works for the good of those who love him, who have been called according to his purpose.

"It says *all* things," continues Brunell. "So even if I don't win a Super Bowl as a starting quarterback. Or if I go through bankruptcy, I may not like it, and it may be the toughest thing I've ever gone through, but it's for His purpose, even if I don't know what that might be yet."

The Brunells were still struggling to complete the bankruptcy and get back on their feet that summer. Most of the debts were personal guarantees on millions' worth of commercial loans that he'd invested in real estate and development partnerships that went bad during the recession. Brunell's partners went bankrupt first, and he shouldered the payments himself until it became too much.

Brunell says he can count on one hand the number of bad decisions he made that got him into financial trouble, including picking bad advisers earlier in his life. But there is no going back now. And there is no questioning God's plan, he says. Only seeking what lessons He wants Mark and his family to learn from it.

"I really believe there is a lot of good that's going to come out of this and there's going to be an opportunity whether it's helping my kids or helping a teammate or using the stuff I'm going through to make a difference in the lives of other people.

"I don't know *what* I'm going to do after football, but I know *who* I'm going to do life with. My wife and my children. We're part of a church in Jacksonville, Florida. My best friend's down there, Tony Boselli, and our kids' friends are down there. I heard it said once that when you find your people you'll find your purpose. And I really believe that. I've found my people. I know who I want to spend the rest of my life with. As far as the job, I don't know what I'm going to do. I trust that God has a plan for us."

SECOND CHANCES

Jerome McDougle, a former first-round draft pick out of the University of Miami, was sitting in his silver Mercedes coupe waiting to meet a friend a few days before the start of the Philadelphia Eagles' training camp in the summer of 2005 when a boy in his early teens approached his window and asked if he could use his cell phone.

McDougle, a 6-foot-3, 260-pound defensive end, didn't feel threatened. It was just a boy. But he wasn't about to give his cell phone to a kid who could run off with it either. "I thought he was joking at first," admits McDougle. "Are you serious? Get out of here."

That's when it happened.

"I felt the cold steel of the gun on the back of my head, and I got chills," said McDougle, who had suddenly found himself surrounded by three teens with handguns. "It didn't seem real," he says. "It was happening so fast, but it felt like everything had slowed down. These were just kids, and a lot of them think you walk around with a million dollars in your pockets. So this looks easy to them."

The boys were exposed, and they were getting angrier by the second. McDougle sat still as they cursed him with four-letter words and promised to shoot him in the head if he didn't "give it up." But there was nothing to give up. He had a few bucks in his pocket, the car . . . there wasn't much else.

This wasn't going as planned, and the kids were obviously getting agitated. The ringleader spotted Jerome's watch, a birthday gift from his brother, Stockar, a Miami Dolphins offensive tackle, who had been selected by the Detroit Lions in the first round of the 2000 draft out of the University of Oklahoma. "Give it up," he said, pointing to the watch. McDougle did as he was instructed, hoping to satisfy them. But it wasn't enough. And that's when it happened.

The boy opened the door, and they fired from point-blank range.

"I heard four shots," McDougle recalls. "One hit me in the stomach, and I leaned into the car, and then I heard three more. Two went in my door, and one shattered the window. I couldn't hear because of the loud bang from the gun. I couldn't see because of the flash of the gun."

The bullet entered his left side, traveled across his body, and lodged under his right pelvic bone. He said he didn't feel any pain initially; the adrenaline had kicked in, and his body was numb.

McDougle didn't pray for his life. He didn't think about the NFL. He didn't reach for his phone to call an ambulance. Instead, he got angry. All he could think about was getting his hands on those boys who shot him. And so he leapt from the car and began chasing the kids down the street. It must have been an odd sight indeed. A couple of kids running for their lives, each holding a gun in his hand, while a 260-pound NFL lineman chased them down the street with blood streaming from his midsection.

A few blocks later, the boys had dispersed down side streets, and McDougle, starting to feel a warm sensation in his stomach, became woozy and collapsed on the sidewalk. Someone called an ambulance, and McDougle lay there thinking about his then two-year-old son Jerome III. "I remember dreaming about him, thinking about his life. The images were flashing before me. I never thought I was going to die. And that's the funny thing about it. Death never entered my mind. Not once. I wasn't willing to concede. I refused to give up."

A CHRISTIAN UPBRINGING

Jerome grew up in Pompano Beach, Florida, the youngest of Linda and Jerome McDougle's four children. The kids attended the Church of God in Christ since they were small. Church was as much a part of being a McDougle as getting a bath. Grandmother Jewel Kelly and mother Linda McDougle, a high school home economics teacher, enforced the children's religious education. But he was still just a kid. And for Jerome, the Bible was something he had been taught and could even recite from, but it was still more of a guide than a commitment. It wasn't until he was into his NFL career that Jerome would gain a greater understanding of what it meant to really commit to Christ.

"Like a lot of kids, I was going through the motions," McDougle reflects. "I was doing it because that was how I came up. But I didn't have a genuine relationship with Jesus that I needed to. It's sort of like Randy Moss when he doesn't want to play hard. You know he's real good, but he's not really playing up to his potential; he's just going through the motions. That's what I was doing, just going through the motions. I would go to church, read my Bible, pray, but I was really doing it because it was what I saw at home; it was what I saw my parents and grandparents were doing. I really didn't have a true relationship with God."

McDougle's experience wasn't that much different from the experience of most young people. What does a relationship with God look like when you are fifteen? Most kids can't get along with their parents at that age and think a "relationship" is what you have after a make-out session in the backseat of a car. Try tackling what it means to have a real relationship with a Creator who doesn't walk in the room and talk to you. So as McDougle continued going to church and reading the Bible, he also began developing into a pretty fine ballplayer.

He started his college football career at Hinds Community College in Raymond, Mississippi, where he developed a close relationship with defensive coordinator Jeff Terrell, and they would attend church together.

"I took another step in my faith and stopped going through the motions and started thinking more about what things meant. But I was still doing things unbecoming of a Christian; stuff like drinking and parties and women and all those types of things," McDougle says. "But I had a better relationship with God then than ever before. At that point in my life, I got saved every other Sunday, you know? They would invite us to Christ. 'Come up now and give your life to Christ.' I did it every weekend, and I felt like I was saved, but I also knew I hadn't completely committed to doing the right thing. I was saved, but I wasn't walking in my liberty. You never really think about the consequences and how it makes God feel. I still enjoyed to party, and I still enjoyed the women."

McDougle dominated at the junior college level, registering 64 tackles, 12 quarterback sacks, and 3 fumble recoveries in 1999, before transferring to the University of Miami in Coral Gables, Florida, in 2000. He helped Miami beat Nebraska 37–14 to finish the season undefeated and win the national championship following the 2001 season.

His senior year, the Hurricanes returned to the national championship, but lost to Ohio State in double overtime, 31–24. McDougle had 55 tackles and 7 quarterback sacks that year. He also was a finalist for the Lombardi Award, given to the nation's best defensive lineman.

In Miami, McDougle connected with team chaplain Steven Caldwell, who became his spiritual leader.

"It was another step to developing a true understanding and love of Jesus," says McDougle. "I was kind of living my life, and he was the one who taught me that, 'OK, just because you make a mistake, that doesn't mean you are not saved or that God doesn't love you. You have to repent and turn away from it.' I was starting to mature and think more about my actions. Maybe I was just getting the partying out of my system."

What McDougle was experiencing was par for the course, explains Caldwell, who has been the Hurricanes' chaplain for more than sixteen years. Miami has had its fair share of top-caliber athletes, accompanied by all the evils that follow their celebrity. Caldwell says all students away from home for the first time face the temptations of sex, drugs, and gambling, but what sets the athlete experience apart is the "illusion of entitlement."

There are invitations to the best parties. The prettiest girls want to be by their side and in their beds. Businesses in the local community might offer everything from cars to clothes at discount prices. The fans just seem to give, give, give . . . at first.

"What happens is that the student-athletes start to believe they are entitled to all of these different perks because of their success," Caldwell says. "That in itself is a trap because they don't see what they have as a privilege. They see it as something they are entitled to because they are stronger and faster and more special than everyone else.

"I tell the guys, 'When you look at yourselves in the mirror, you have to ask yourself, "What did I do to be as good as I am?" Is it that you trained hard, fought through adversity, did repetition after repetition? Well, really that's something you did to maintain your gift. You woke up one morning and discovered that you had something very special that you didn't ask for: extraordinary size, speed, balance, touch, vision—it was all given to you at birth. And do you know who gave that to you? It was given to you by God. You are not entitled to this; it is a gift that has been bestowed upon you.'

"I remember once asking [former San Diego Chargers Pro Bowl linebacker] Junior Seau, 'What's it like to be you? What did you do so well that God blessed you?'"

Caldwell asks athletes, including McDougle, these questions because he wants them to develop a sense of humility. They didn't work any harder than millions of high school athletes who spent their off-seasons lifting weights, running sprints, catching passes, and dreaming that someday all their hard work would land them in the pros. The difference isn't the effort. That's like telling a kid that if he works a little harder on his multiplication tables, he might someday become a mathematics savant. Either you're born with it or you're not. God has given all of us some special gift; the challenge is figuring out what it is.

In the meantime, they are tempted by the gifts and the attention, and few are mature enough to turn it away. They struggle to see the implications of the freebies, Caldwell says.

"Initially, it's great. That's how it is if you are a great player, right? You get stuff. People love you, man. This is the big time. You've worked hard for this, and this is part of the reward, right? What they don't see is that the people giving them things are trying to position themselves to take from them later on. They are going to want something in return eventually."

According to Caldwell, it all circles back to the illusion of entitlement. "It causes you not to think about later," he explains. "The illusion convinces you not to plan for the future because you are always going to be who you are, and it will always be at this level. You are not thinking about the implications ten years into the future. It's always going to be this way."

It was conversations like this one that started connecting the dots for McDougle. By the time McDougle started his senior year at Miami, Caldwell had seen a significant change in his mental state. McDougle had always been a jokester, but now he was beginning to understand his own potential and the opportunity he had to advance to the next level. His brother Stockar had already been drafted by the Detroit Lions, and Jerome was starting to take his life a little more seriously, Caldwell says.

It was coming together a little at a time. But McDougle was still partying and being promiscuous. The school chaplain preached balance and took the approach that it's a lot easier to minister to someone who is listening than to someone who has shut you out of his or her life.

"I believe if you are too religious, you can be a judgmentalist. But if you don't have a strong enough relationship, you can become a compromiser," Caldwell continues. "I teach them how to have a balanced life. Just because you follow Christ doesn't mean you have to disassociate yourself with people who don't believe as you do. You can be a light amongst the darkness."

Caldwell, who later married McDougle to his wife, Jaceinte, with whom he now has four children, believes McDougle found that balance in his life and his true calling to Jesus Christ the day he escaped death in his bullet-riddled Mercedes coupe.

"Some people take it as a badge of honor, as street cred," Caldwell says. "But Jerome saw it as a moment to reflect on his relationship with the Lord."

FIGHTING FOR HIS LIFE

An ambulance was called, and McDougle was airlifted to Jackson Memorial Hospital's Ryder Trauma Center in Miami. The immediate surge of adrenaline that had allowed him to ignore the pain had dissipated, and no matter which way he turned, he couldn't get comfortable. He was bleeding internally, which, as he describes it, is "a pain that you can't put into words." McDougle's career was hanging in the balance, but football never entered his mind.

"I remember one of the guys saying to me, 'Are you with me? Stay up.' And I was like, 'Man, I'm not going anywhere. You don't have to worry about me. I'm here. I'm not going anywhere. I'm up, and I'm going to stay up.'"

At this point in his life, Jerome had taken a series of steps in his walk with God. As a boy, he was following his parents' instructions and doing as he was told. This set a foundation for him to lean on later in his life, he says. During his high school and college years, he loved God, read the Word, tried to live a righteous life, and asked for forgiveness when he sinned. But he was still choosing *when* to be a Christian and was conflicted by his desire to do what was right by God and his own personal demons that ached for the nightlife.

When he reached the NFL, he felt that he was maturing as a man and was starting to truly understand the importance of his faith, of making a commitment to Christ and passing his beliefs down to his children. Yet his experiences in the NFL, along with the shooting, would show him that he still hadn't completely turned his life over to Christ. Sometimes, he says, we have to be brought to our knees and forced to consider God in a way we might not have without a crisis. The next several weeks and months of his life, McDougle would learn this lesson.

PARALYSIS

When McDougle came out of surgery, he couldn't walk. The doctors explained that the bullet was lodged under his pelvic bone and was pinching a nerve. Trying to get it out could do more harm than good, they said, so the doctors decided to leave it in and wait and see if, in time, he would regain the use of his legs.

This was the first time Jerome's thoughts turned to his NFL career. If you can't walk, you can't chase quarterbacks. And if you can't chase quarterbacks, what good are you to the team? The doctors were honest and direct. They told him that he'd probably never play football again.

"That was the first time I got the feeling that something I loved was going to be taken away from me. It was scary. It was very real. I couldn't move my legs. But that's also when you find out what you got inside. And there was this little part of my mind that was listening to them, but was like, 'I know me better than anybody, and I'll beat this.'"

The rehabilitation was painful, but he recovered much more

quickly than anyone had imagined. There was no movement at first. Then, in time, he could deal with the pain enough to walk across the room. Then, he was back in the weight room, and by the fourth week of the season he was ready to return to the team.

"It's funny how the enemy does; he kicks you when you are down," McDougle says.

The Eagles had traded their 2003 first- and second-round draft picks to the San Diego Chargers to move up fifteen spots where they could select McDougle with the fifteenth overall pick. They signed him to a six-year, $12.6 million contract that included an upfront signing bonus of $6.1 million, according to the *New York Times*.[3] All that was left for their first-round draft pick was to turn on the jets and start causing havoc with opposing offensive fronts. But McDougle's five-year career with the Eagles was marred by one injury after another, not to mention the shooting.

In 2003, ankle, hip, and knee injuries kept him out of eight games. In 2004, he was diagnosed with an irregular heartbeat that kept him out of one game, followed by a knee sprain that sidelined him the final four games. In the weeks leading up to the 2005 training camp, Eagles coach Andy Reid commented that McDougle had worked hard during the off-season and looked better than ever. This was going to be the year everyone had been waiting for. Instead, he was shot and nearly lost the use of his legs. And just when you'd think his life couldn't get any worse . . . it did.

"I was running and training and doing martial arts to strengthen my core strength, and I was stronger than before I got shot," McDougle says. "I joked that I had iron in me [the bullet], which is why I was so strong. And it was literally a week from returning to practice when a terrible pain hit me.

"This pain was so awful. I can't put it into words. It brought

---

3. http://www.nytimes.com/keyword/jerome-mcdougle.

me to my knees, and I couldn't talk. I thank God my wife was there because she called the ambulance."

Doctors discovered that he had a rupture where an incision had been made during the operation following the shooting, and his intestines had pushed through. That's bad, but the pain wasn't bad enough for Jerome to notice. What gave him the awful pain was that it had gotten infected and turned into gangrene. The doctor told McDougle that if he had waited another day, he would have been dead from the infection. Instead, they scheduled emergency surgery and cut out the infected portion of his intestine. He would live, but the season, the one in which Reid thought McDougle would live up to his expectations, was over.

Jerome was emotionally wiped out.

He'd taken his God-given abilities, trained them, and climbed the ladder to the game's highest level. He'd had injuries, but fought through them and was confident that he would eventually live up to his potential and become the NFL player he was capable of. No, he couldn't see the shooting coming. But he gutted it out, refused to quit, and was ready to return to the game in better shape than before the incident. Then . . . gangrene? To quote tennis player John McEnroe, "You can't be serious!"

McDougle didn't know which way to turn. He's always found the positive in bad situations, he says. He's lived a pretty faithful life, even if during his youth he didn't live up to God's expectations, and he felt closer to God in 2005 than he'd ever felt in his life. He was born again—and again and again and again, he says. Why was this happening when others with much lesser skills and commitment to God were apparently succeeding and living their dreams? He didn't know where to go.

"After that [the gangrene] happened, I'm praying, and I asked God, 'Why?' But I decided that I need to trust in God even more. It was to the point that, where else are you going to go? It's like the question that Jesus asked Peter when people were leaving Him. He said, "Are you going to leave too? And Peter said, 'In Your hand is eternal life.' And I was at that point. I had nowhere else to go, so I had to turn to God and trust in Him. I couldn't try to fix things on my own anymore. I kept fighting back, refusing to quit and accept defeat, and I kept getting knocked back down. I had no choice but to trust in God. I told myself that I could have been stuck lying in bed without the use of my legs for the rest of my life, but God helped me up. So He must have had a plan for my life, right?"

Jerome wasn't alone. He had family and friends walking from room to room in his home, praying for God to watch over him. Jerome was anxious and knew he needed God's help. But he felt guilty too. He says that he had been using God as a spare tire in his life and that this experience was the push he needed to make a life-time commitment to leading a Christian life.

"You only take the spare tire out when you need it," he says. "As long as you are riding smooth and comfortable, everything is good. You got the top down, your hair in the wind, the sun on your face, but as soon as you get that flat tire, as soon as an issue comes in your life you want to pull out that spare tire, you want to pull out God. You learn as you mature to not use God as a spare tire. It's *His* plan, not *your* plan."

"I'M GLAD I WAS SHOT"

If this was a screenplay, now is about the time when the hero in our story would overcome his injuries and rise to become the All-Pro he was destined to be just as the credits are starting to roll. But that's not how it would be for Jerome McDougle.

Jerome sat out all of 2005 as he recovered from the injury and its complications. The following year he was lost for three games with fractured ribs. And in 2007, he tore his triceps in the preseason and was placed on injured reserve.

When the Eagles finally gave up and released him at the end of their 2008 NFL training camp, he'd played in a grand total of thirty-three games, registering 29 solo tackles and 3 quarterback sacks. He signed a free agent contract with the New York Giants a short time later. But for all intents and purposes, it was the end of his NFL career.

"As I've studied [the Bible] more, I've learned that with experience there lies power because you have that testimony and experience to draw from," McDougle says. "I think God uses our experiences, good as well as bad, to bring us to a point where you are walking in your calling. I thank God for going through that experience because I know it's made me stronger in my faith and in Him because it put me in a position where I had to trust in God. And now I am walking in my true calling.

"They opened fire on me from point-blank range. I don't think they were bad shots. I think there was a divine purpose for me to survive that shooting. I know God had His hands over me just enough to get me to a point where He could use me."

McDougle was born with the gifts Pastor Caldwell talks to his players about at the University of Miami. "The great privilege," he calls it. And McDougle worked hard to develop and maintain those tools to advance to the highest level in the game. And just when he was ready to put his gifts to work and become the dominant player the Eagles thought he would become, it was all taken away from him either by injuries or by a deadly assault. No matter how many times he got back up, he kept getting knocked back down. And then it was over. Just like that.

You might think that McDougle would be angry. It was that raw emotion that led him to chase those boys down the street with a gunshot wound and blood streaming from his abdomen. It was that anger that motivated him to battle back, train, and recover from the injuries and the operation and the complications. But when it all ended, he didn't feel anger at all. He was on his walk then, and he knew he wasn't alone anymore.

"Think about the children of Israel," McDougle says. "Look at all the people they had to fight before they got to the promised land. If great things are just given to you, you don't appreciate it. If God had just taken them to the promised land, they'd still be worshiping other gods and having orgies . . . because they wouldn't have developed the purpose in their lives that came to them through their hardships. God takes you through life with all its ups and downs because you need it. It's all to help you fulfill your purpose, to use your testimony to help someone else and bring other souls to God.

"I have a story now. I can give my testimony to young people so that it may guide them down a better path. I grew up in a tough area where a lot of my classmates are dead or in prison. I was shot and survived it. I lived a life in college that God didn't want me to lead. I've experienced injuries and struggles in the NFL. Your testimony is not for you; it's for someone else to learn from what you've been through. I think that God's plan for me is to help others avoid making the same mistakes I made. It's not about me."

McDougle, who is returning to school to get his master's in business administration, is sure God's plan for him is about helping others, particularly college athletes and those new to the NFL. He has been working with the NFL's player engagement office, which helps players from the time they enter the league through their retirement.

McDougle said he's learned to trust in God and to understand life is about His plan, not our plans. Jerome likes to share a few words of wisdom he received from his brother Stockar.

"My brother always tells me, if you want to make God laugh, tell Him your plan. If you want to do right, get in the backseat and let Him drive."

And that's what McDougle believes he is doing—letting Christ drive.

9

WHAT IT MEANS TO LEAD

*A dispute also arose among them as to which of them was consid-
ered to be greatest. Jesus said to them, "The kings of the Gentiles
lord it over them; and those who exercise authority over them call
themselves Benefactors. But you are not to be like that. Instead, the
greatest among you should be like the youngest, and the one who
rules like the one who serves. For who is greater, the one who is at
the table or the one who serves? Is it not the one who is at the table?
But I am among you as one who serves."*

—Luke 22:24–27

Every world leader, every battlefield general, every captain of
industry was a kid who turned to his or her friends once and
said, "Let's go to the park and throw the football." . . . "Let's go to
the creek and skip rocks." . . . "Let's go to the corner and get an
ice-cream cone." Then, after a few confident steps, they looked over
their shoulders to see if their buddies were following.

Leadership isn't something that is bestowed by titles, pro-
nouncements, or proclamations. Leadership is determined by the

willingness of the people who choose to follow because they believe they are being led somewhere good, prosperous, safe, or fun.

Too often, today's managers forget to look over their shoulders. And when it becomes clear they are traipsing off alone, they resort to shouting, threatening, whipping, and using other methods to prove their power of persuasion. Do you know anyone like this? Have you ever had a boss who believed that leadership was the ability to order others to obey his or her commands whether they made sense or not?

The Bible teaches us that leadership is all about servitude. We are most Christlike when we serve others, who in turn see the benefit of our leadership and follow us. It is an ideal grounded in the belief that we have a responsibility to God and the creatures He put on earth. It is not a gateway to our own personal glory or financial gain, though He sometimes rewards us in this earthly way.

Perhaps nowhere in our daily lives is leadership more on display than on an athletic field, where our greatest heroes are endowed not only with tremendous God-given talent but also with the humility and devotion to team goals that allow them to stand out among some of the greatest athletes of our time.

SERVANTHOOD

Baltimore Ravens linebacker Ray Lewis is one of the most feared linebackers to have ever played the game. Over a sixteen-year NFL career, all in Baltimore, he has been voted to thirteen Pro Bowls, has twice been named the NFL's Defensive Player of the Year, and was Super Bowl XXXV's Most Valuable Player.

While he's received plenty of accolades for his on-field performance, he's made some mistakes in his life too. He had children out of wedlock, and he didn't always choose the best friends. In February 2000, Lewis was charged with murder after two men were stabbed to death in a street fight outside an Atlanta nightclub following that year's Super Bowl. He was exonerated of the murder charges, but not until after he'd been dragged before the public in shackles and faced the possibility of life in prison for a crime he didn't commit. It forced him to take a hard look at the people he was hanging out with.

Through the ups and downs and growing pains and all the celebrity pitfalls, Lewis maintained a resolute faith in God—one that had been instilled in him by his mother, Buffy Jenkins, as a child. It would be his support system during the worst of times and serve as a reminder of his calling to serve God in those moments when the world chose to put him on a pedestal.

More than anything, Ray Lewis will likely be remembered as one of the NFL's greatest leaders of men, both on and off the football field.

Seated on a small stool in front of his locker a few days before the start of the 2011 play-offs, Lewis is asked to explain his leadership style and to identify those who are most important in teaching him how to be a leader. He pauses for a moment and then recites Mark 9:35:

> Sitting down, Jesus called the Twelve and said, "Anyone who wants to be first must be the very last, and the servant of all."

For the Ravens' inside linebacker, it all began in the mid-1980s at Greater Faith Missionary Baptist Church in Mulberry, Florida, where he was a junior deacon. He would attend Bible studies, take up tithes and offerings, and help out where he could. Most of his family members attended the church—his cousins were in the choir—and the congregation took notice of how mature little Ray's prayers were. He was only eleven or twelve, but it was obvious he was reading the Bible and grasping its stories.

"My grandma and great-grandma would come and say, 'God's got His hands on you,'" Ray remembers.

When you are a child, such words from an admired adult make

you beam with pride. It's the sort of memory you carry with you later in life. And it's something Lewis would remember years later as teammates began to come to him for a word or a line of scripture when they had lost their way.

He understood because like a lot of us, he, too, had lost his way from time to time. The celebrity of being a star football player from high school through the pros can be intoxicating, he says. And even though he'd had a proper religious upbringing, the women, the parties, the false friends proved too tempting in his youth.

"We all get away [from our faith] for a minute, but the Good Book says you raise up a child the way they should be raised and when need arises they'll come back," Lewis says. "That's the thing Mom instilled in me very early. God is your backbone. He is your resource. He is your confidant. So when you are young and you are going through [difficulties], the thing I learned is to never take a break from God—good, bad, ugly, shameful."

Lewis was drafted by the Ravens out of the University of Miami with the twenty-sixth overall pick in the 1996 NFL draft. He was a dynamic player from the start and quickly developed a reputation for being a high-energy, high-impact player, capable of standing up to a 300-pound tackle and or sending a fullback flying backward.

Lewis sprinted everywhere, and by his sheer desire to get to the ball, he put himself in position to make plays whether he was making the tackle, recovering a fumble, or intercepting a tipped pass. If he didn't make the first hit, he'd drive the pile back a step or two or three when he arrived half a second later.

In no time, the accolades began rolling in: AFC Defensive Player of the Week, All-Rookie Team, Linebacker of the Year, Pro Bowl.

Lewis was learning the pro game, and his athletic talents and work ethic allowed him to do it faster than most. It was the first stage of developing into the leader he would eventually become, he says.

Lewis says there are four steps to becoming a leader, whether you work in an NFL locker room or at the local bowling alley. First, master your craft. Second, help others. Third, share the Word. Fourth, live what you are preaching so that you will be heard and others will know it to be true and genuine.

"A job title doesn't define a leader. What you do [for a living] doesn't define a leader," Lewis says. "It doesn't matter how many Pro Bowls I've gone to. It doesn't matter whether I go into the Hall of Fame. None of that defines a leader.

"To be a leader, you've got to be willing to serve others. Learn your job and become excellent at it. Then seek to help others. As they improve and benefit from your assistance, they will see the wisdom in it and will look to you for guidance and leadership again. It's not enough to be great at your job. If you don't serve others and genuinely seek to make everyone around you better, your talent won't matter. Practice your craft, then help those around you," he encourages.

This is true on the field, but also in your faith, Lewis adds. Jesus was a leader who confessed with His mouth that His Father is our final Maker, the beginning and the end. And when He was persecuted for that, He said, "I will still confess with My tongue that You are My Father."

In any environment, you rarely see someone confessing his or her faith, Lewis says. That's what creates spiritual leadership. When someone sees how strong your faith is, that's what makes people want to follow you outside of the workplace.

"Be good at your job, help others, confess your faith, back it up with the way you live," Lewis says. "But what comes first? Servitude. And we see that in Jesus. All He did was serve, from the lowest of lows. Remember, He was a carpenter."

Perhaps no passage in the Bible demonstrates the importance of servanthood to a Christlike life as clearly as John 13. The scene begins with the Passover feast where Jesus and His disciples are gathering for a meal. At the time, it wouldn't have been out of the ordinary for a servant to wash a guest's feet following a long journey and before they sat down for dinner. There were none on this day, and you can only imagine the disciples getting a little peeved and looking around for *someone* to do the job.

In today's world, it might equate to the way office workers sometimes stand around waiting for the janitor to show up and rearrange the desks before a meeting or a group of people watching a busy waitress rush around getting orders while they wait for someone to bus their table. Who among us would get up and help rather than wait for the servants?

It was just before the Passover Festival. Jesus knew that the hour had come for him to leave this world and go to the Father. Having loved his own who were in the world, he loved them to the end.

The evening meal was in progress, and the devil had already prompted Judas, the son of Simon Iscariot, to betray Jesus. Jesus knew that the Father had put all things under his power, and that he had come from God and was returning to God; so he got up from the meal, took off his outer clothing, and wrapped a towel around his waist. After that, he poured water into a basin and began to wash his disciples' feet, drying them with the towel that was wrapped around him. . . . When he had finished washing their feet, he put on his clothes and returned to his place. "Do you understand what I have done for you?" he asked them. "You call me 'Teacher' and 'Lord,' and rightly so, for that is what I am. Now that I, your Lord and Teacher, have washed your feet, you also should wash one another's feet. I have set you an example that you should do as I have done for you. Very truly I tell you, no servant is greater than his master, nor is a messenger greater than the one who sent him. Now that you know these things, you will be blessed if you do them." (John 13:1–5, 12–17)

In practical terms, when the best player on the team is willing to serve his teammates by sharing his experience, instructing a rookie on a technique, or lending an ear when he sees someone struggling in his personal life, it shows that he realizes that in God's eyes, he's no better than anyone else, no matter how much money or fame society bestows upon him. And that's a powerful thing to those who see themselves as not having the same amount of power or prestige or respect. Jesus Christ Himself, knowing that He was the Son of God, emphasized this when He washed His disciples' feet.

Is this sort of behavior—where our leaders serve the weakest members in order to make the whole stronger than its individual parts—something we see demonstrated very often in society?

Do we see it in our political leaders? How about our corporate executives? Or our police force? And what is our personal responsibility in encouraging this behavior in our local neighborhoods and places of work?

> *Since an overseer manages God's household, he must be blameless—not overbearing, not quick-tempered, not given to drunkenness, not violent, not pursuing dishonest gain. Rather, he must be hospitable, one who loves what is good, who is self-controlled, upright, holy and disciplined.*
> (Titus 1:7–8)

Lewis has an enormous following in Baltimore. Fans clamor to get his autograph, and media refer to him as the face of the franchise. He is one of the most recognized and sought-out players throughout the NFL and is always the television networks' key pregame interview, where he is usually referred to as a "future Hall of Famer."

It would be easy for Ray Lewis to believe his own press clippings. But he says that if you maintain a desire to serve other people, and therefore God, it "steps in the way of selfishness" because you are too busy trying to help others instead of basking in your own glory and success. No one wants to follow a supposed leader who cares more about himself than his followers. And don't think those followers and God Himself aren't watching and judging all the time.

"When you find yourself in these workplaces, whether you are copying documents or you are a garbage man, what is your interaction when you cross somebody's path?" Lewis asks. "What do you make them feel like? Good, bad, sad, indifferent—what does your spirit give off?"

But Lewis says that great leadership goes beyond just performing well individually and helping those around him. To be a true leader, he says, a player must also embrace his faith and be willing to confess it to others.

"When you think about true leadership, you're not talking about *man* giving leadership. If you focus on that alone, then you will judge yourself by the way systems see you, by the way other men see you. Live so that people surrounded in darkness, when they see you, you light up their darkness."

For even the Son of Man did not come to be served, but to serve, and to give his life as a ransom for many. (Mark 10:45)

Former Denver Broncos quarterback Tim Tebow became a lightning rod in 2011 when his game-day prayers and postgame comments about his love of Jesus were portrayed as over the top and out of place in the world of professional football.

The former Heisman Trophy winner from the University of Florida defended his Christian beliefs and said God had given him and every other celebrity athlete a stage to speak to millions about the role He plays in our daily lives. It was too important an opportunity to let slip through his fingers, he says.

Tebow was attending the John Lynch Salute the Stars luncheon in Denver when he was asked about leadership. The video was posted to YouTube on May 15, 2011. Though his comments were directed toward other NFL players, listen to his words and apply them to your life and the interactions you have with the people in your house and community:

> All leadership is, is someone, who someone else is looking at; who someone else will follow. So honestly, I'm not the only leader up here. Every single one of you are leaders because someone is always watching. Yes, as a quarterback and a football player, you have a bigger platform to reach more people, and I take that responsibility and obligation to heart; and honestly how I play and I live off the field, I want to be a good role model for kids.
>
> Unfortunately, today there aren't enough great role models playing in the NFL. So it's my goal and my passion to be a great leader for the kids in this community and the kids all over.
>
> I get so sick when I hear the athletes say, "I'm not a role model." Yes you are, you're just not a very good one.[1]

IS A BOSS A LEADER?

Heath Evans was selected by the Seattle Seahawks in the third round of the 2001 draft out of Auburn University. He played for Seattle, Miami, New England, and New Orleans before retiring after the 2010 season and now works as an analyst for the NFL Network.

Evans, who served as the New England Patriots' ministry leader after their pastor retired, says the core principle of servant leadership is, unfortunately, looked at backward in today's culture.

"People think leaders are, 'You do this . . . You do that.' That's their idea of the *boss*. But true leadership is seen in guys like [Patriots

---

1. http://www.youtube.com/watch?v=OHlQTGLDWIM.

coach] Bill Belichick, [Saints quarterback] Drew Brees and [Patriots quarterback] Tom Brady," whose leadership style mimics that of Jesus Christ, whether they know it or not.

The focal point of the Bible is Jesus Christ. He came to earth and died so that anyone who chooses to believe in Him can have life. He did all the work, and we get all the gain, Evans says.

"When I look at Drew Brees, I see a guy who sacrifices his family, his time, his diet . . . everything he does is for the betterment of the team on the field and in the community. All the sacrifices he makes to try and create an edge benefits him, but it's really for the team. And they see that."

Sports teach so many lessons that help a child when he or she becomes an adult. Leadership, self-discipline, how to keep your mind clear and focused when under stress, never quitting, bouncing back from defeat . . . but perhaps none is more important than the way it instructs us to develop the qualities of leadership: execution, servitude, humility, spiritual guidance, genuineness.

Winning is important, but consider that NFL quarterbacks complete only about 61 percent of their passes. National Basketball Association players convert only about 46 percent of their field goals. And in baseball, players who fail to get a hit 70 percent of the time are named to the All-Star team.

Even the very best players in professional sports require a cadre of support staff, talented teammates, and a smart front office. Try finding a star quarterback with a horrible offensive line or a great linebacker without a talented nose tackle protecting him from blockers.

Furthermore, try finding a great editor without a staff of talented reporters or a terrific dentist without a team of good hygienists.

"There is a success that comes from being a humble leader or even a humble superstar," Evans says. "Both of these guys [Brees and Brady] are the most humble superstars I've ever been around in my life.

"Yes, they work for their own gain. But ultimately, each guy works in a fashion where they always have the team at heart. Brady and Brees could care less whether they throw the ball thirty-five times or twenty times, as long as they win. A lot of quarterbacks in this league, well, that's not the way they are," he says without identifying them.

Though Tebow hasn't had nearly the on-field success of Brady or Brees, his behavior exemplifies what Evans and Lewis are referring to when they speak about making personal sacrifice and putting others first.

Consider Tebow's postgame comments after the Broncos' 13–10 overtime victory over the Chicago Bears on December 11, 2011, in Denver. Tebow converted 21 of 40 passes for 236 yards and led the team back from a 10-point deficit late in the game to set up Matt Prater's 51-yard game-winning field goal.

> I just want to thank Coach Fox and the coaches for giving me the opportunity and believing in me for the entire game and for the defense for keeping us in it and our receivers and our offensive line, who at the end of the game made me look a lot better than I really am.
>
> But guys kept encouraging one another, defense kept encouraging offense; the offense encouraging special teams. Just try to keep believing until the very end. It wasn't looking very good, but guys kept, shoot, encouraging me, at all times, believing in me, and we kept believing, and I think that's special when you have a team that believes and a team that's going to continually fight for sixty minutes, even though it's not looking good and even though it might be frustrating.
>
> We might have had opportunities and missed them, but we kept fighting and kept going, and the defense played phenomenal and came up with a bunch of huge stops, and we were finally able to get a drive there and score—a bunch of guys stepped up on that drive; the offensive line protected great, and D.T. stepped up on that drive; and Jeremiah and Lance and Deck, and a bunch of guys

really stepped up, and we were able to get the ball back and find a way to go down there.

At certain times in the game where I was very frustrated and disappointed. Obviously, I thought we had opportunities—we had opportunities for the lead—so it was disappointing we were down 10–0. But great things are only possible if you're under very tough circumstances. That was a great comeback for this team, and it was led by our defense and coaches and a team that constantly believes.

If you believe, unbelievable things can sometimes be possible. I think that's pretty special that we have a team that constantly believes and believes in each other.

In both word and deed, Tebow was the consummate team player. And while his performance was up and down at times, he earned the love and loyalty of his teammates because they knew him to be genuine in his beliefs and resolute in his commitment to the team. Though his religious beliefs put Tebow in the public eye, behind the scenes, he didn't seek special favor like many celebrity athletes.

Do nothing out of selfish ambition or vain conceit. Rather, in humility value others above yourselves. (Philippians 2:3)

Top coaches demonstrate leadership in a similar way, Evans says. When their team has success, they praise the team. And when they fall short, they always beat themselves up and feel like they let their players down.

This is because leadership isn't about having more money or a bigger house or fame. It's about having more responsibility. Not just for yourself anymore, but for the whole group. And while that might come with perks, the leader's responsibility in a team's failure is greater than any one man's.

"All these attributes are biblical core principles," Evans says.

"'Humble yourself and lift up other people' . . . 'to whom much is given much is required.'"

According to Evans, these players and coaches say, "Hey, I've been blessed with a lot of talent and ability, and I need to use it for good."

"I think about what they do in their communities," Evans continues, "and [how they] use the platform to impact so many lives. The core principles of Christianity are what make true leaders. People don't want to be barked at and told what to do. Ultimately the greatest leaders I've been around, they set the tone about what is the right way to do things by putting all the lessons into action for us to see."

Evans preaches to kids that it's better to be respected than liked. He says that in the Christian faith, many people fall into the trap of trying to be perfect, and that's not what the Christian faith is. He tells them that respect comes from being genuine in their beliefs, being humble, and by acknowledging that they aren't perfect.

"Throughout the Bible, God knew we would never be good enough, and that's why He sent Jesus. So when I messed up, I was the first to apologize. If I acted out with a coach, I was in his office apologizing the next morning. I'm not perfect. I'm trying to live life right, and sometimes I fail. But I think I'm living a life worthy of respect."

It's about accountability, he adds. Leadership requires that we are accountable to ourselves, our co-workers, our managers, our beliefs, and our God.

New York Giants defensive end Justin Tuck can relate to Evans's experience. Tuck is one of the best pass rushers in the league, but he is human and doesn't always feel like a superstar on the inside or behave like the perfect Christian on the outside.

He says that when people are thrust into leadership roles, it can sometimes be overwhelming. How many of us have attended a class at our place of business or had a discussion with our manager on the subject of leadership? Probably not many. Further, most managers would probably not know what to say if asked.

Raw talent or success at a particular task is hardly enough preparation to lead others. This is why players like Lewis and Aaron Rodgers and Evans speak of the value servitude plays in molding leaders.

"Sometimes you get caught up in being a leader," Tuck says. "But what does that mean exactly? How do you do that? It doesn't mean that I don't go out there and make enemies or miss tackles or I'm the greatest thing since sliced bread. My faith has taught me how to follow. And I don't think you can be a great leader without first knowing how to follow.

"Talent has a lot to do with leadership, but I know guys who have great talent who don't show up for meetings on time or are not accountable. If you want to be a leader, you have to be the guy who runs to the ball at practice, who does the little things because everyone is watching you. Leadership is more about doing than talking."

Tuck says that motivating other teammates requires a leader to understand them at a personal level. Some guys respond well when a leader yells or gets in their faces. Other guys respond better when he pulls them aside. And there are still other personalities who respond best when he quietly says, "You know what? I'm going to help you in this situation by showing you how it's supposed to be done."

Tuck adds, "If they see me doing the little things, then they say, 'That's our leader. He's a seven-year vet. He's won accolades. He's won a Super Bowl. If he can do these things, maybe he has it figured out.'"

Tuck says his faith has molded him as a man. And it's that personal side, rather than his talent as a Pro Bowl player, that allows him to do the most good with his co-workers.

"You see a guy is struggling, and you just go up and have a conversation with him," Tuck said. "It doesn't have to be about the Bible.

You just have to show them that you genuinely care about them or have a care for how their lives are going. That comes from the Word and learning to love each other. That's part of leadership too.

"We talk about this all the time in Bible study. All of us have a purpose in life, and even though I play football, my purpose isn't to be a football player.

"My success comes from knowing I am trying to live the life that God has wanted me to live. Sure, it comes with Pro Bowls, new contracts, and a Super Bowl ring. But I can't take any of that with me. When my days here are done, I can't give my testimony to the Lord and Savior and say, 'Ah, You know, God, I had a few sacks in my career. That's got to get me somewhere, right?'"

Sometimes, leadership also means taking a stand for your beliefs, no matter how much criticism you might receive. Outside football, that can mean defending a co-worker who is being treated unfairly or standing up to a bully in the boardroom who is trying to force his views on others with threats and other forms of persuasion.

In November 2011, former Denver Broncos quarterback Jake Plummer was being interviewed by XTRA Sports 910 in Phoenix when he mentioned that he wished Tim Tebow would pull back on all the references to God. It was a complaint many Christians and non-Christians alike had of the quarterback during the 2011 season.

Tebow spoke to ESPN's *First Take* the next day and was asked to respond to Plummer's comments:

> If you're married, and you have a wife, and you really love your wife, is it good enough to only say to your wife "I love you" the day you get married? Or should you tell her every single day when you wake up and every opportunity?
>
> And that's how I feel about my relationship with Jesus Christ is that it is the most important thing in my life. So anytime I get an opportunity to tell Him that I love Him or am

given an opportunity to shout Him out on national TV, I'm gonna take that opportunity. And so I look at it as a relationship that I have with Him that I want to give Him the honor and glory anytime I have the opportunity. And then right after I give Him the honor and glory, I always try to give my teammates the honor and glory.

And that's how it works because Christ comes first in my life, and then my family, and then my teammates. I respect Jake's opinion, and I really appreciate his compliment of calling me a winner. But I feel like anytime I get the opportunity to give the Lord some praise, He is due for it.

Tebow shows the same willingness to stand up and fight for what he believes spiritually as he does when he's staring down the toughest defenses the NFL has to offer.

Sometimes it takes more courage to stand up and fight for the Lord in front of a nation than it does to run over a 250-pound linebacker for a first down. Tebow attacks his role as a leader on the field and as a child of God with the same tenacity.

> *The greatest among you will be your servant. For those who exalt themselves will be humbled, and those who humble themselves will be exalted.* (Matthew 23:11–12)

BLESSINGS FOR THE FAITHFUL

The 2011 football season proved to be a spectacular one for some of the league's most faithful players. After a four-month lockout that canceled minicamps and shortened training camp, the league's thirty-two teams came together to produce one of the most outstanding offensive performances the league has ever known. And some of the league's most recognized Christians were among those leading the way.

The Saints' Brees passed for an NFL single-season record 5,476 yards, breaking the twenty-seven-year-old record held by former Miami Dolphins quarterback Dan Marino. He helped New Orleans put up a league record 7,474 total offensive yards. And Brees was voted to his sixth Pro Bowl after leading the Saints to the postseason for the third consecutive year, including their only Super Bowl title after the 2009 season.

Baltimore's Ray Lewis led his team in tackles (95), was voted to his thirteenth Pro Bowl, and recovered from a foot injury in time to lead the Ravens into the play-offs for the fourth consecutive year.

Tim Tebow came off the bench to lead the Broncos to five fourth-quarter come-from-behind victories, helping them qualify for their first postseason berth since 2005. Then in the first-round game against the Pittsburgh Steelers, he threw for a season-high 316 yards, including an 80-yard touchdown strike to Demaryius Thomas on the first play of overtime to notch the victory, 29–23.

But perhaps none of them had as good a year as Green Bay quarterback Aaron Rodgers, one of the NFL's best passers and most devout Christians. He led the Packers to a 31–25 victory over the Pittsburgh Steelers in Super Bowl XLV in February and was named the game's Most Valuable Player, completing 24 of 39 passes for 304 yards and three touchdowns.

The Packers returned to the play-offs in 2011, after finishing the regular season with a near perfect 15-1 record. Rodgers was even better, passing for a personal best 4,643 yards and 45 touchdowns and was voted the league's Most Valuable Player.

Rodgers, like Lewis and Tuck and so many other fantastic Christian NFL players, led by example through the way he provided leadership during the long, arduous NFL season.

Though his words come from the lips of an NFL star, they speak to all of us no matter our race, our age, our gender, or the profession God has chosen for us to pursue.

"I've always lived by the philosophy of the words spoken by St. Francis of Assisi who said, 'Preach the gospel at all times, if necessary, use words.' I feel like you can always have a greater impact by the things you do than the things you say, so living out my faith has been primarily in that form," Rodgers said before the Packers opening play-off game.

"I think it helps to have a pretty good knowledge of the way that Jesus spoke and taught and interacted with people in the New Testament. He cared about people, He spent time with people, He cared about relationships, and that's kind of my leadership style. I want to get to know the guys. I want to have relationships with them. I want there to be that connection because I really feel like team chemistry is an underrated part of a team's success. Having that tight-knit feel with your teammates and trying to let your actions speak louder than your words—that's how I've chosen to lead."

ACKNOWLEDGMENTS

Writing a book is a lot like building a skyscraper. It takes years of planning and is impossible to complete without the knowledge and support of hundreds of capable hands. In the end, one man gets his name on the plaque outside the front door.

Here is where we attempt to rectify that injustice.

This book, which took six years from conception to publication, was made possible by all the players, players' wives, coaches, team executives, and chaplains who were generous enough to share their stories of faith and football.

Though I spoke to more than one hundred sources for this book, I'd like to give special thanks to San Diego Chargers chaplain Shawn Mitchell and Washington Redskins chaplain Brett Fuller, whose insights were essential to organizing the project. I'd also like to give special thanks to coaches Andy Reid, Tony Dungy, Chan Gailey, Mike Singletary, and Marvin Lewis for their candor. They didn't hold back, even though they are in the public eye and knew they might be criticized for their beliefs. Players Matt Hasselbeck, Ray Lewis, and Justin Tuck gave me time during the 2011 season when they were at their busiest, allowing me to peek behind the curtain and challenge some of the notions of what it means to be a competitor and leader. Former player Troy Vincent was one of the good guys during his playing days. He now works for the league office and was especially honest about the struggles players face in transitioning out of the NFL. Trent Dilfer, one of the best NFL analysts on television, went above and beyond in retelling me of the death of his son, Trevin. It was heartbreaking to hear him relive the most painful experience of his life. We both cried during that interview. Thanks, Trent. And I'd like to say a special thanks to a group of people who often go unnoticed. They are the men and women in the NFL's thirty-two public relations offices who regularly arrange interviews, make requests on our behalf, and take calls at all hours of the day and night to help us check the facts. I can't tell you how many times I received an email from one of them at 10:00 p.m. or even midnight. You are essential to the job we journalists perform, and we don't say thank you nearly often enough.

At the outset, it was my co-worker and good friend Cary O'Reilly who read my story on former Washington Redskins coach Joe Gibbs and encouraged me to pursue this project. Naturally, I told him he was crazy. But over time, Cary convinced me that the project could have an impact beyond just the football field and that it could change my life in ways I might not imagine. He was right, and I appreciate his decision to ignore, pester, and ultimately cajole me into writing this book. Co-worker Vince Golle, another good friend and a former editor of mine at *Bloomberg*, has always been a steadying influence. I can be emotional at times. Vince knows this, and he'd sit quietly letting me get it out, then ask a simple question that would immediately lead to greater clarity and oftentimes an *aha!* moment. Vince read several chapters and performed early edits of my work, deleting extraneous anecdotes and scripture and helping me hone in on the players' messages. My old roommate Jessica Vasquez, now a sociology professor at the University of Oregon, provided assistance with some early research when I was formulating my idea.

Of course, the book didn't become a reality until *Bloomberg* editor-in-chief Matt Winkler signed off on the project. I worked at *Bloomberg* during the days and researched and wrote the book in the evenings and every weekend for a year. During that time, I received support from *Bloomberg* executive editor John McCorry, managing editor Jay Beberman, and sports editor Michael Sillup. I am indebted to them all.

My wife, Judit, is my partner in life. As with most of my work, she is the first to read and provide edits. She is my confidante, my ego builder, my reality check, and the one person who always believed in me, even when I didn't believe in myself.

My brother, Brian, helped me research scripture that was suitable for certain passages. Literary agent Howard Yoon was my professor at Georgetown University during graduate school and agreed to serve as my literary agent. It was Howard who found the good people at Thomas Nelson, namely, publisher Matt Baugher and editor Adria Haley. Without a steady, confident, honest editor, no work is worth publishing.

Last, thanks to all my family, my friends, and those players, some of whom never made it into the book, who offered their support and who showed me how it's possible to work hard, compete fairly, and still live a Christian life.